MW01170940

LOVE MAKES THE

WORLD

GO ROUND

Also, by Taliba Lockhart

White Light:
The Eye View of God

Invisible Shield:
Safely in His Arms

Joy And Gladness:
Even in the Midst of your storm

Meeting God:
A Divine Personal Encounter

LifeLine:
He Hears our Desperate Cry

I Am A Witness:
Unquestionable He Lives

It's So Beautiful:
For it is Finished

God's Blessed or Happy Life:
How to Attain It

Love Makes the World Go Round:

For God So Loved

For further information please contact
Taliba Lockhart @ tallock48@gmail.com
or visit my author's page
www.amazon.com/author/talibalockhart

Unless otherwise indicated, all scripture quotations are taken from the *New King James Version Bible.*

*Love Makes The World Go Round; For God so Loved"
"You shall love the LORD your God with all your heart, with all your soul, with all your strength, and with all your mind,' and 'your neighbor as yourself'" (Luke 10:27).*

Made in USA
February11, 2022
ISBN 9798351536750

Acknowledging the absolute True and Living God. Every book I have written is filled with amazing testimonies; my soul intention is to point the reader to the Almighty, Loving Creator in the hope that you may come to know Him one day soon.

LOVE MAKES THE

World

GO ROUND

For God So Loved

By Taliba Lockhart

Table of Content

GOD IS CALLING US TO LOVE MORE.

Dedication

This book is dedicated to those who thirst and hunger for God, and to those who are starving for love. You see, in this world people souls are starving for love but they don't realize that's the problem. God revealed that to me one night in 1998 as I sat at my desk writing my first book; He arrested my attention as I heard Him say, *"I sit on my throne; I see throughout the whole world every problem and every situation. I see the needs, the desires of my suffering souls. I see my souls dying of starvation, starvation of love."*

So, this book is dedicated to all those who are feeling unfulfilled in their heart and soul–longing to be fulfilled, satisfied, whole and complete. God can and wants to filled that empty void with His presence; as a matter of fact, God is the only One Who can. This book is also dedicated to those suffering and dying of starvation, starvation of love. Not only will God give you His precious love, He will also give you peace that passes all understanding—causing you to feel complete, whole and satisfied. Thus, you have a need to get to know your Creator, God, and His Son, Jesus Christ, your Lord and Savior. God wants you to know how much He loves you; then He wants to equip or train you to love others more.

Introduction

Introduces The Power of God and His Unconditional Perfect Love for His Children

My reason for writing *Love Makes the World Go Round* is to introduce, on another level the true and living God's wonderful, unfailing and unconditional love for His children; as well as acquaint us with an in-depth view of His magnificent, awesome and glorious power and control He has over the world events. Many times, we can act like Job– thinking we know God, when in reality we don't know Him like we think we know Him. However, the most important reason for this book is to let others know how seriously important it is to the God of the universe that we let Him in our hearts, that we may truly learn to love one another as He loves us all; for He is our ultimate Lover!

1 John 4:8 says, *"He who does not love does not know God, for God is love."* Have you ever wondered why some people couldn't care less about not wanting to know their God and Creator? He Who magnificently flung the stars, hung the sun and moon on nothing in the great atmosphere and the universal firmament: (the sky, air, heaven, space, vaults and azure blue). Spun the Solar System into orbit, right down to

hanging the earth, and everything on it and in it—including the many nations of people–on nothing! We are literally hanging out in space on nothing! How can something like that be so awesome? Man couldn't have done it!

Do you, or anyone you know believes it all just happen to happen one day by chance out of the blue? If so, something or someone had to caused it to happen! Who or what do you think it was? Don't answer! There has to be an Infinite Mind full of Wisdom, Power and Love to bring it into existence. There has to be an All–knowing, All–seeing, All–powerful and Everywhere Supreme Being Who Created it all, and is holding it all together by the power of His Word, His Spirit and His love, which is the Bond of Perfection. There has to be an All-Sufficient Self-Existing Source, God Himself Who is the Sovereign Ruler of the Universe! What's more, He not only created the universe and is holding it together, but He is sustaining it because He so Loved the world: It's truly His Love that Makes the World go Round. Listen to what His Word says in Jeremiah 51:15, *"He has made the earth by His power; He has established the world by His wisdom, And stretched out the heaven by His understanding, or at His discretion."*

We need to know we serve an awesome and mighty God; the real true and living God of the universe, and there is none like Him in all the earth. He is the Almighty and the Great I AM. He is greatly to be praised and greatly to be feared. I am afraid many of us just do not know, love and fear

God enough. In Psalms it says, *"Great is the LORD, and greatly to be praised; And His greatness is unsearchable. For the LORD is greatly to be feared above all gods" (Psalms 96:4, 145:3).* Job says this about God. *"Behold, God is mighty, but despises no one; He is mighty in strength of understanding. With God is awesome majesty. As for the Almighty, we cannot find Him; He is excellent in power, In judgment and abundant justice; He does not oppress. Therefore, men fear Him; He shows no partiality to any who are wise of heart" (Job 36:5, 37:21-24).* So, let's be wise in heart and mind and believe He exist–because He does exist! We must learn to see God with our mind's eye or with the eyes of our spirit or inner man. If He didn't exist, why would He so adamantly proclaim these marvelous things of Himself?

"For every beast of the forest is Mine, And the cattle on a thousand hills. I know all the birds of the mountains, And the wild beasts of the are Mine. If I were hungry, I would not tell you; For the world is Mine, and all its fullness" (Psalms 50:10). "...For I am God, and there is no other; I am God, and there is none like Me," (Isaiah 46:9). "I am the LORD, and there is no other; There is no God besides Me. I will gird you, though you have not known Me, That they may know from the rising of the sun to its setting That there is none besides Me. I am the LORD, and there is no other; I form the light and create darkness, I make peace and create calamity; I, the LORD, do all these things" (Isaiah 45:5-7). "I have made the earth, And created man on it. I, My hands-stretched out the heavens, And all their host I

have commanded" (Isaiah 45:12). "… Thus says the LORD, who stretches out the heavens, lays the foundation of the earth, and forms the spirit of man within him" (Zechariah 12:1). Thus says the LORD, your Redeemer, And He who formed you from the womb: "I am the LORD, who makes all things, Who stretches out the heavens all alone, Who spreads abroad the earth by Myself; (Isaiah 44:24).

David praised God by saying, *"O LORD, our Lord, How excellent is Your name in all the earth, Who have set Your glory above the heavens" (Psalms 8:1)!* The Apostol Paul said this of God, *"For by him were all things created, that are in heaven, and that are in earth, visible and invisible, whether they be thrones, or dominions, or principalities, or powers: <u>all things were created by him, and for him: And he is before all things, and by him all things consist,</u> (Colossians 1:16-17).* Wow! All things! God is before <u>all</u> things, and by Him <u>all</u> things consist. Thus, <u>everything</u> entails or involves Him.

Let's learn a little more about our magnificent God through His answers to His servant, Job, when Job was contending with God; justifying himself rather than God. You see, Job was blameless and upright, a righteous man of integrity. He feared God and shunned evil. Job had great possessions; he was the wealthiest man in the East, but he lost everything he had. Job suffered greatly with painful boils from the sole of his foot to the crown of his head; even his wife told him to curse God and die. Job was accustomed to accepting adversities along with the good in life. Thus, he held fast to his faith. Throughout Job's terrible suffering he maintained his integrity and asserted his innocence. However, Job decided to confront God with question that he might vindicate or defend himself because he was a righteous man before his God—and wow, did God answer Job! God's answers will not only captivate your attention, but will also fascinate your mind. God answered Job by asking him these tough questions:

> *"Who is this who darkens counsel By words without knowledge? Where were you when I laid the foundations of the earth? Tell Me, if you have understanding. Who determined its measurements? Surely you know! Or who stretched the line upon it? To what were its foundations fastened? Or who laid its cornerstone, When the morning stars sang together, And all the sons of God shouted for joy? Or who shut in the sea with doors, When it burst forth and issued from the womb; When I made the clouds its garment, And thick darkness its swaddling band; When I fixed My limit for it, And set bars and doors; When I said, 'This far you may come, but no farther, And here your proud waves must stop. Have you commanded the morning since your days began, And caused the dawn to know its place, That it might take hold of the ends of the earth, And the wicked be shaken out of it?" (Job 38:2-13).*

My, What a God! *"Have you entered the*

springs of the sea? Or have you walked in search of the depths? Have the gates of death been revealed to you? Or have you seen the doors of the shadow of death? Have you comprehended the breadth of the earth? Tell Me, if you know all this. Where is the way to the dwelling of light? And darkness, where is its place, That you may take it to its territory, That you may know the paths to its home? Do you know it, because you were born then, Or because the number of your days is great? Have you entered the treasury of snow, Or have you seen the treasury of hail, Which I have reserved for the time of trouble, For the day of battle and war? By what way is light diffused, Or the east wind scattered over the earth?" (*Job 38:16-24*). Wow, God is the Great One here. I don't know about you, but I would have to answer, Lord, You know.

"Do you know the ordinances of the heavens? Can you set their dominion over the earth? Can you lift up your voice to the clouds, That an abundance of water may cover you? Can you send out lightnings, that they may go, And say to you, 'Here we are? Who has put wisdom in the mind? Or who has given understanding to the heart? Who can number the clouds by wisdom? Or who can pour out the bottles of heaven, When the dust hardens in clumps, And the clods cling together?" (Job 38:33-38). *"Have you given the horse strength? Have you clothed his neck with thunder? Can you frighten him like a locust? His*

majestic snorting strikes terror. He paws in the valley, and rejoices in his strength; He gallops into the clash of arms. He mocks at fear, and is not frightened; Nor does he turn back from the sword." (Job 39:19-22). "Does the hawk fly by your wisdom, And spread its wings toward the south? Does the eagle mount up at your command, And make its nest on high?" (Job 39:26-27).

Then finally, God asked Job this question. "Shall the one who contends with the Almighty correct Him? He who rebukes God, let him answer it" (Job 40:2). Then Job answered the LORD and said: "Behold, I am vile; What shall I answer You? I lay my hand over my mouth. Once I have spoken, but I will not answer; Yes, twice, but I will proceed no further" (Job 40:4-5). God's questions for Job continues.

"Would you indeed annul My judgment? Would you condemn Me that you may be justified? Have you an arm like God? Or can you thunder with a voice like His? Then adorn yourself with majesty and splendor, and array yourself with glory and beauty. Disperse the rage of your wrath; Look on everyone who is proud, and humble him. Look on everyone who is proud, and bring him low; Tread down the wicked in their place. Hide them in the dust together, Bind their faces in hidden darkness. Then I will also confess to you That your own right hand can save you" (Job 40:8-14).

Then God goes on to say, *"Look now at the behemoth, which I made along with you; He eats grass like an ox. his strength is in his hips, And his power is in his stomach muscles. He moves his tail like a cedar; The sinews of his thighs are tightly knit. His bones are like beams of bronze, His ribs like bars of iron. He is the first of the ways of God; Only He who made him can bring near His sword (Job 40:15-19). "Can you draw out Leviathan with a hook, Or snare his tongue with a line which you lower? Can you put a reed through his nose, Or pierce his jaw with a hook? Will he make many supplications to you?* God's questions continue.

Will he speak softly to you? Will he make a covenant with you? Will you take him as a servant forever? Will you play with him as with a bird, Or will you leash him for your maidens? Will your companions make a banquet of him? Will they apportion him among the merchants? Can you fill his skin with harpoons, Or his head with fishing spears? ... Indeed, any hope of overcoming him is false; Shall one not be overwhelmed at the sight of him? No one is so fierce that he would dare stir him up. Who then is able to stand against Me? Who has preceded Me, that I should pay him? Everything under heaven is Mine. (Job 41:1 11).

My, my, my; how great and awesome is our God! Job answers the Lord once again. *"Then Job answered the LORD and said: I know that You can do everything, And that no purpose of Yours can be withheld from You. You asked, 'Who is this who hides counsel without knowledge?' Therefore, I have uttered what I did not understand, Things too wonderful for me, which I did not know. Listen, please, and let me speak; You said, 'I will question you, and you shall answer Me.' I have heard of You by the hearing of the ear, But now my eye sees You. Therefore I abhor myself, And repent in dust and ashes" (Job 42:1-6).* I agree with Job–none of us know God like we think we know Him! **Bless us O' Lord not only to hear You with our ears, but also see You with our mind's eyes.**

Wow! Glory be to the Almighty God! He is worthy to be praised, greatly to be feared! How overwhelmingly, powerful, wonderful, brilliant, superb, and marvelous is our God in all His amazing and astonishing works: Words cannot even begin to express how excellent and spectacular God is, and neither can our minds fathom all His Greatness, or understand all the mighty works He has done. If we could comprehend the mind of God, we would be God: He is much too infinite. However, it is unquestionably clear that He is ruling and reigning from above. He is so High and Holy, yet, He is so meek and lowly–He thought of wretched man, and loved us enough to send His Holy Spirit to dwell within us while we are here on earth.

When we think about how Great and good God is–we should wonder why we want to keep our minds filled with bad and fearful news continually? Keeping our minds stayed on Him will keep us from worrying so much about all the negativity that is going on in this present world. But we need not think for one minute with all that is going on in the world that God is not in total control, because He absolutely is. Most of us just need to get to know our Creator/God better by trusting in Him, believing in Him and studying His Word. Start by Reading the book of Job and the first book in the Bible, Genesis. If you are not convinced that God is real— may the loving God who created you have mercy upon your soul and reveal Himself to you. Don't waste your time trying to prove He doesn't exist, use your time wisely proving He does exist, because He truly does exist; just don't wait too long before you finally do find out, because then it may be too late!

This old song comes to mind when talking about the Love that makes the world go round. Do you remember the song *"What The World Need Now is Love, Sweet Love?"* It was true then and it is absolutely true today! The next line goes on to say, *"No, not just for some, but for everyone."* That statement is definitely ringing truer today, than then. For so many are still not treated with the love God has commanded us to show toward them. In Romans 13:8 the Bible says, *"Owe no one anything except to love one another, for he who loves another has fulfilled the law."* From the looks of what going on in our world today, we have not yet fulfilled that law.

I believe many people misery and unhappiness stems from hatred harbored in their hearts for others; just as many people's misery or unhappiness stems from feeling unloved, because of maltreatment due to injustice by the powers that be—who could actually change certain conditions but refuse not to. Many others are miserable and unhappy because they feel or believe they have been forsaken or abandon by the ones they love. But God wants People to know today how much He loves them, and how precious they are to Him. They need to be assured that He will never abandon or forsake them. God wants to love them through us. Are you opened to allow God to love others through you?

God said, *I will never leave you nor forsake you"* (*Heb13:5*). Nothing shall be able to separate us from God's love. The great Apostol Paul said, *For I am persuaded, that neither death, nor life, nor angels, nor principalities, nor powers, nor things present, nor things to come, nor height nor depth, nor any other created thing, shall be able to separate us from the love of God which is in Christ Jesus our Lord. (Romans 8:38-39)!* Hopefully this book will open people up to the love of God, so they may be able to love others more; because we are all God's creative choice, made in His image, and He has commanded us to love one another! What will you do about it?

In 1995 when God, the Creator of the world first came into my life He taught me many things. One thing in particular I will never forget. He said these words to me one day during my devotion time with him. He said, ***"Source, is where all things originate from. I am the Source of all things. Love is deep, deep in your soul where all meaning for life is formed. You are formed out of deep love."*** I never forgotten those words. So, our Father is a God of deep love and He has formed us out of that deep love. Thus, He has given us the directive, or command to love one another. That's how important Love is.

Not only do we all need to be loved, but we all were formed and created out of deep love. God gave us the capacity to love one another—definitely not to hate one another as we see demonstrated so prevalently today—coming from some people toward other people. Why is it that way? Simply because some people do not know the true and living God. Or, they have simply chosen not to retain God in their mind—thinking they don't need Him. Some choose not to believe in Him: Others even think they are <u>God</u> themselves. If a person chooses not to believe in the God Who created them, who do they believe in? Bottom line, there are only three choices, Self, Satan or God! Just remember every knee will bow and confess to God one day, including Satan. Romans 14:11 says, *"For it is written: "As I live, says the LORD, Every knee shall bow to Me, And every tongue shall confess to God."*

No matter who you are, or what color you are, or what your status in life is, or where you live, or what you have or do, or who you think you are; if you do not have love in your heart toward others, you are nothing! That's why Paul stated in I Corinthians the 13th chapters that it's good to have gifts, but it does not matter about all the gifts one may have or how well they used their gifts—without love—the gifts profits little. The Apostle Paul placed much emphasis on people striving and seeking after the greatest gift—Love. For loving others is a more excellent and better way of life; for a lifestyle of loving others surpasses all other lifestyles.

Therefore, if we want to profit, let us strive for genuine love to rest in our heart for others. When we open our mouth to speak to others, we want our words to profit them; we do not want to become as sounding brass or a clanging cymbal (I Corinthians .13:1). Even if you have the gift of prophecy, and understand all mysteries and all knowledge, and have all faith so that you could remove mountains, but have not love, the Bible says, you are nothing (I Corinthians 13:1-2).

So then, it is of great necessity that each of us learn to love others and learn to live a peaceful and contented lifestyle as God would have us to. Thus, we must have a personal relationship with our God at the forefront of our lives, because without God in our lives it will be impossible for us to love others as we should, simply because GOD IS LOVE and Love comes from God. Without Him in us, we cannot experience genuine love for others and neither will we be able to live in true joy and peace.

The greatest commandment Jesus spoke of in His days on earth is just as true today as it was then. In Mark the 12-Chapter, verses 28–31, one of the Scribes asked Jesus concerning the commandments—he asked, *"Which is the first commandment of all?" Jesus answered him, "The first of all the commandments is: 'Hear, O Israel, the LORD our God, the LORD is one. And you shall love the LORD your God with all your heart, with all your soul, with all your mind, and with all your strength.' This is the first commandment. And the second, like it, is this: 'You shall love your neighbor as yourself.' There is no other commandment greater than these."*

So, you see how important it is for us to have love for one another. We must remember God so loved the world that He gave His only begotten Son to die, not only for our sins, but for the sins of the whole world—ALL PEOPLE: red, yellow, black or white, rich or poor, educated or uneducated. We are all precious to Him, because He loves all His children the same. None more favorite or special than another; for we all are individually His favorite and special child. No one of us is without fault or sin. NO NOT ONE! Romans 3:23 says, *"For all have sinned and fall short of the glory of God,"* So No One is exempt, for No One is all that special or important: especially if you do not love, and cannot forgive others. Paul has a lot to say concerning the boastful big-headed people who think they are better than others and have something to brag about. Or they may feel they are more worthy than others, or that only they deserve special treatment; while others should be treated unfairly, unjustly and unequal; while others are just plain overlooked.

Listen to the words of the Apostle Paul. He said, *"For if anyone thinks himself to be something, when he is nothing, he deceives himself. Not that we are sufficient of ourselves to think of anything as being from ourselves, but our sufficiency is from God. And if anyone thinks that he knows anything, he knows nothing yet as he ought to know. But if anyone loves God, this one is known by Him,".* (Ga 6:3, 2Co 3:5, 1Co 8:2-3). Amen! Does God know you? Let's not think too highly of ourselves than we ought.

Thus, whoever any of us are—know you would be nothing and neither could you do anything without God! Jesus said, *"...for without me you can do nothing (John 15:5).* We all are God's choice. No one, but no one is better than anyone else. If you think you are, Satan has severely deceived you and blinded your mind to the truth, because *God shows no partiality* to no one, TO NO ONE! (Acts 10:34). I feel the same way the Apostle Paul felt when he said, *"But from those who seemed to be something--whatever they were, it makes no difference to me; God shows personal favoritism to no man--for those who seemed to be something added nothing to me"* *(Galatians 2:6).*

However, many have hatred and detestation in their hearts, and have shown partiality, favoritism and disrespect toward other men all throughout history simply because of the color of their skin, their slanted eyes, their high cheek bones, the texture of their hair, their thin lips, or their broad noses. I say this to those who have shown hatred, injustice, unrighteousness, disrespect and partiality toward other men— you need to know—you are worse off than those you hate, because you do not love. You also need to know, **God loves all people the same, and if you don't believe He does, and you think you are better you most definitely need to repent and ask God's forgiveness' and Read His Manual, the Holy Bible. Pray for understanding and that your eyes may see, your mind be enlightened and your heart be reassured of God's unconditional perfect love for all His people.** God never intended for man to rule over another man in an unfair, unjust and indecent way, and neither did God intend for men to hate other men; but on the contrary He intended for man to get to know one another, respect one another, be merciful, show compassion and love to one another.

One need to understand just how powerful and loving our God really is. He loves us with an everlasting love and He is the All-Encompassing-Spirit. He encircles and surrounds the entire creation. In Him we live and move and have our being (Acts 17:28). He is One Spirit in all human beings. God cannot be dichotomized, because God is Spirit and Spirit cannot be divided or split up into parts and pieces. God is One Spirit and His One Spirit is in all of us. That's why He wants us to love each other. Did you know when you show love to another you are showing love to God? God said to me once, *"I AM that I AM,"* meaning, He will be what He wills to be and

He has willed His One Spirit to be in all of us and in all things. He is Omni, which means "All:"

We need to know that God loves diversity or variety. He is the Potter and we are the clay. He has created us all uniquely and exceptionally differently by His own design. *"But now, O LORD, You are our Father; We are the clay, and You our potter; And all we are the work of Your hand" (Isaiah 64:8).* Paul said we all are God's creation or handiwork, those who are created in Christ should be walking in good works which were ordained for us before we came to know Christ. *"For we are his workmanship, created in Christ Jesus unto good works, which God hath before ordained that we should walk in them, (Ephesians 2:10).* In other words, God wanted our actions and motives to always glorify Him.

He is **Omnipotent,** which means He is all-powerful. He has unlimited power and authority. He has all ability to do as He pleases. He is the authority; He doesn't have to ask for authority. He answers to no one, but everyone answers to Him–or will answer to Him one day, because God is still in charge. Listen, *"But indeed, O man, who are you to reply against God? Will the thing formed say to him who formed it, "Why have you made me like this?" (Romans 9:20).* Can you see we are no more special than anyone else is, and that God does as He pleases.

He is **Omniscient,** which means He has all-knowledge. He knows everything, and He knows everything about everyone, and He knows everything everyone knows. Remember God's answers above to His servant Job. He keeps watch and knows all our thoughts and deeds. Listen, *"The eyes of the LORD are in every place, Keeping watch on the evil and the good" (Proverbs 15:3)*. So, we better be good for heaven's sake. Selah. We may not see all the evil others do, but please know, God does; for His eyes are always watching us. Listen, *"The eyes of the LORD are in every place, beholding the evil and the good" (Proverbs 15:3)*.

He is **Omnipresent,** which means He is present everywhere at the same time. He lives all over and within the entire universe. He lives in and all around the cosmos. He stands still and is everywhere. There is no where we can be, that He is not there! Listen, *"And there is no creature hidden from His sight, but all things are naked and open to the eyes of Him to whom we must give account" (Hebrews 4:13)*. So, we will have to answer one day for our behavior. These words are true, and they are God's Words, not mind. Listen, *"Hell, and Destruction are before the LORD; So how much more the hearts of the sons of men" (Proverbs 15:11)*. Selah (think about it). God sees what's in our minds and our hearts, as a large print open book.

Our God is Awesome, Magnificent and Great and He is God all by Himself. None can compare to Him. He is the total, absolute truth: He is unquestionably Living and Real! Yes, our God is one God, one Spirit and one Truth, even though God's one truth can look many different ways, or have many different levels, heights, planes or stages. Paul says it this way, *"But we all, with open face beholding as in a glass the glory of the Lord, are changed into the same image from glory to glory, even as by the Spirit of the Lord. ... becoming more and more in knowledge after the image of Him Who created us,"* (II Corinthians 3:18, Colossians 3:10). In other words, we are constantly growing or changing from "*glory to glory,*" or from level to level becoming more and more like God in our nature and character. If we are not very careful to keep an open mind, we might not know the truth when we see or hear it. Just thinking of God's Grandness should cause us to humble ourselves before Him, and start giving the world more of what it needs, "Love, Sweet Love; no, not just for some, but for everyone!"

LOVE:
I Corinthians 13 Chapter 1–8

"1 Though I speak with the tongues of men and of angels, but have not love, I have become sounding brass or a clanging cymbal.
2 And though I have the gift of prophecy, and understand all mysteries and all knowledge, and though I have all faith, so that I could remove mountains, but have not love, I am nothing.
3 And though I bestow all my goods to feed the poor, and though I give my body to be burned, but have not love, it profits me nothing.
4 Love suffers long and is kind; love does not envy; love does not parade itself, is not puffed up;
5 does not behave rudely, does not seek its own, is not provoked, thinks no evil;
6 does not rejoice in iniquity, but rejoices in the truth;
7 bears all things, believes all things, hopes all things, endures all things.
8 Love never fails. But whether there are prophecies, they will fail; whether there are tongues, they will cease; whether there is knowledge, it will vanish away."

Love makes the World Go Round

Chapter 1

We Must Have Love

…"Though I speak with the tongues of men and of angels, but have not love, I have become sounding brass or a clanging cymbal," (I Co 13:1).

Jesus left with us these words, *"Love one another."* Just what is this that's called 'L*ove*'? Love is deep because it entails much. So, let's see how the dictionary defines the word *"love."* Definitions reads as follows, **1**. *"The meaning of LOVE is strong affection for another arising out of kinship or personal ties.* **2**. *Love is a set of emotions and behaviors characterized by intimacy, passion, and commitment. It involves care, closeness, protectiveness, attraction, affection, and trust.* **3**. *A feeling of kindness or brotherhood toward others.* **4**. *An intense feeling of deep affection for another.* **5**. *God's mercy and benevolence toward humans.* **6**. *Humankind's devotion to or adoration of God."* And **7**. *deep affection, fondness, tenderness, warmth,*

1

intimacy, attachment, endearment, devotion and adoration." These definitions sum up how many of us feel toward those we care deeply about, and how others feels toward us, and how we should feel toward our God and Creator.

Now, not to have love–and open our mouth speaking to others we will sound as a sharp ringing, which is to make excessive noise, having nothing inside us that will contribute to their spiritual welfare. Whereas, love to God and men is the best gift which God bestows, and we all should earnestly desire, seek and cherish love in ourselves and for others. Because if we do not have the love of God, and love for mankind filling our hearts, the words we proclaim will not be heard, but fall by the wayside.

Therefore, since we need, and must have *"Love"* let's take a closer look at the word *'Must.'* Must, is similar to a command or request; it means, essential, requirement, necessity, obligation, prerequisite or duty. In other words, *'Must'* is a qualification you must have to get to where you want to go. The Bible teaches us that God is LOVE. I John 4:8 says, *"He who does not love does not know God, for God is love."* If we honestly want to know Who and What real 'Love' is, then we have a vital and crucial need to get to know who our God and Heavenly Father is. I John 4:16 says *"...He who abides in love abides in God, and God in him."* Now the questions are, do you know your God? Do you love your God?

2

Whatever your answer is, whoever you are, you should know that God has made known that He loves you unconditionally. The Bible says, *"In this the love of God was manifested toward us, that God has sent His only begotten Son into the world, that we might live through Him" (1 John 4:9).* Another well-known and often quoted scripture says, *"For God so loved the world that He gave His only begotten Son, that whoever believes in Him should not perish but have everlasting life" (John 3:16).* So, God has definitely proven how much He love us by sending His Son to die for our sins—even while we were still in our mess, that we might live a better life.

Truly loving others like God loves us opens the door to that abundant life. That's why Love is a necessity and Love is the greatest of all the fruit of the spirit, and we would do well to seek it above all else. Many have the ability to speak elegantly and articulately, but even if we could speak all the languages in the world, our voice would be heard with little or no value to God, if we do not have love in our hearts for God and our fellowman. Worse yet, the Bible says we would become *as sounding brass or a tinkling cymbal,* without soul or feelings, sounding worthless in the ears of God—not truly benefiting anyone. That's why Love is a must and a necessity if we want to please our God.

Listen, do you really want to know how God loves you? God love is His unselfish giving of Himself. Who do you think wake you up every morning? Who gives you the strength and ability to work? He loves you unconditionally. He gives us

3

unlimited grace and mercy every day. He forgives our sins. He gives you peace and joy in your heart. He gave us His Son. He has given us a fearfully and wonderfully made body in His own image, with His Spirit inside us. The list is non-stop of what He does for you and me. Don't be deceived–thinking you are the source of your blessing. Now, do you really want to know how you love Him? *He said if you love me, keep my commandments.* He knows you are not perfect, but do you obey Him? (John 14:15). That is how you know if you love Him; you obey Him.

Many are capable of singing like an angel, with the most beautiful voice you ever heard, but to have not love in your hearts toward others, your singing will be hollow noise in the ears of God. You see, Love is the most important thing to God; Love is the reason He gave us His son, Jesus. Thus, in all we do in word or deed, we should do it in the name of the Lord, giving glory, thanks and honor to the Lord, our God. All our motives, actions and intentions should be rooted in Love, and all our ways should be acceptable to our Heavenly Father, and not unto men. As children of God, if we love Him, we should obey Him. We are required to make our lives and ways attractive to Him and it is of great necessity to have a prayer life to communicate with God; as we are to always pray (Ephesians 6:18).

We should pray like David prayed, *"Create in me a clean heart, O God, And renew a steadfast spirit within me. Do not cast me away from Your presence, And do not take Your Holy Spirit from me (Psalms 51:10).* Do you know that David was a man

4

after God's own heart: not because he was so perfect, but because he was merciful to his enemy, Saul, and he always confessed his sins and found time to pray to God? Remember, our words aren't always as important as the attitude of our heart. God looks for a pure hearted person!

I Corinthians 13th and the first verse is telling us we can be well spoken, well-groomed, well behaved and well versed; however, it does not matter to God about our outer appearance, gifts or our talents, if we do not have love in our hearts for our brethren. Whatever we accomplished or accumulated in life, we must know that God did it through us. Whatever organization or company we have influence or authority over, without a sincere heart of love toward others our efforts of services may become hollow; or ineffective. So, demonstrating good character with love is key in God's eyes.

After all is said and done, Matthew 8:36 says, *"For what will it profit a man if he gains the whole world, and loses his own soul?"* Now that's something to think about. That said, then the only thing left for us to conquer is love, becoming more like our God in character. Can you imagine what the world would look like if everyone would just humble themselves and start loving those they just don't like, simply because others are different. Do they not realize that God has made all of us in His own image (Genesis 1:27)? In other words, God has made duplicates of Himself, according to His likeness, according to His characteristics

5

What is God's character, and what should God's character look like in us? God told me once, saying, "Your character is My face; My face is your character." In other words, He was saying my lifestyle, my behavior, my personality, my character, the way I talk and the way I conduct myself should represent Him. Therefore, God's character is His nature: His disposition, His mannerism, His temperament, His pull, His draw, His grace and His forgiveness. More importantly, His character is His unconditional perfect love for His children. Of course, God has many, many more beautiful and wonderful characteristic—too many to list or count here.

The point is that our character should look like love. God wants us to grow in love becoming mature in His character— demonstrating or representing Him to others. He wants us to live our lives in such a way to draw others to Himself. So, wake up you non-lovers and help make the world go round! Start showing love to those you don't know and those you don't like for no other reason, except that God created them uniquely different than He created you! Let your love show mercy to those who need it; be kind, polite and friendly to someone, show compassion to others; do it with genuine love in your heart, otherwise it won't count! You may as well had not done it!

Think about this. We all bleed red blood, we all cry salty tears, we all feel pain, we all use the same number of muscles to smile. We all want to be loved, we all have the same basic body structures, we all use the bathroom, we all eat, we all put on our clothes, and do we all not sleep? We all want the best for our families and for our children to get the best education. And surely, we all want to be treated fairly, justly and respectfully. Loving others shouldn't have anything to do with you being white or my being black, or any other skin color. Or, where we live, or what we have, rather you are rich or I am poor, learned or unlearned—God has freely Loved us all unconditionally and He has given us the command to Love one another.

Truly loving others depending on knowing and loving God, because God made ALL of us in His own image. Listen to this, Then God said, *"Let Us make man in Our image, according to Our likeness; ... So, God created man in His own image; in the image of God, He created him; male and female He created them" (Genesis 1:26-27).* He created us, not in your image, not in my image, but God's own image!

You and I are just another human being like everyone else. No better, no less and no worse; no matter who you are. Remember, God loves diversity or variety in everything and everyone. That's why you see a vast diversity of everything in His creation. Just look around at nature: the different kinds of trees, the different kinds of flowers, fruits and vegetables; and yes, He created even people with different personalities, skin tones, shades or colors too. As a matter of fact, if you really want to know and see what God's skin tone or color is—look at yourself! Selah! Think about it.

We are here on earth in the first place, because God wanted to demonstrate His awesomeness through all of us. He wanted children to love and wanted His children to obey Him, and love Him back–bringing glory and honor to His name; getting to know Him as our God and Creator; learning how to love and accept each other as He accepts us all. More importantly, He needs us to help make the world go round by loving others, as He loves us all. For we are all made in the image of our God, and He did not send us into the world to despise each other, tearing the world apart and pulling it down by allowing the enemy to rule in our lives; neither did God send us here to mistreat one another by treating others unjustly, unfairly and inhumanely. So, drop the hate and pick up LOVE, and shame the Devil! For Love is God, and God is LOVE.

So, you see God has created you and me and everybody else in His own image, and has commanded us to love one another? Listen to the desire of God for us to love one another. *"A new commandment I give to you, that you love one another; as I have loved you, that you also love one another" (John 13:34). "Beloved, if God so loved us, we also ought to love one another" (1 John 4:11)," This is My commandment, that you love one another as I have loved you" (John 15:12). "These things I command you, that you love one another" (John 15:17).*

Paul said, *"Owe no one anything except to love one another, for he who loves another has fulfilled the law" (Romans*

13:8). Isn't it simple, the one thing God requires of us—*"Love one another"* to fulfill the law—but yet, it seems to be the most difficult thing for some of us to do–when all we have to do is stop hating and stop judging others. Jesus said, *"...I judge no man"* (John 8:15). Then He told us not to judge others. He said in Matthew 7:1 *"Judge not, that you be not judged."* If Jesus doesn't judge us, then we truly need to stop judging, criticizing and condemning one another.

In the Bible, in the book of Hebrews the 13th chapter and the 1st verse say, *"Let brotherly love continue."* Paul also tells us to show affection with brotherly love, and to give preference to our brother or sister, saying, *"Be kindly affectionate to one another with brotherly love, in honor giving preference to one another" (Romans 12:10).* Paul continues to teach on love, saying, *"But concerning brotherly love you have no need that I should write to you, for you yourselves are taught by God to love one another" (1 Thessalonians 4:9).* Again, John says, *"For this is the message that you heard from the beginning, that we should love one another" (1 John 3:11). "And this is His commandment: that we should believe on the name of His Son Jesus Christ and love one another, as He gave us commandment" (1 John 3:23).*

The apostle Peter tells us not only to love, but love one another fervently, taking 'love' a couple steps farther than what John said. Peter said, *"Since you have purified your souls in obeying the truth through the Spirit in sincere love of the brethren, love one another fervently with a pure heart".* Honor all people. *Love the brotherhood. Fear God. Honor the king (1 Peter 1:22, 1 Peter 2:17).* Are you a King's kid? Do you really know the king? He is The Ruler. The Almighty Sovereign God of the universe and there is none like Him. He is the King of kings and the Lord of lords. He is the Magnificent Master Who holds the whole world in His hand, and knows the end of things from the beginning.

Then Peter goes onto say, *"Finally, all of you be of one mind, having compassion for one another; love as brothers, be tenderhearted, be courteous;" (1 Peter 3:8).* Our Loving and forgiving God expects us to have a loving attitude toward all people, but especially to those of the house hold of faith. Quoted above, are just a few of the scriptures on loving one another, but there are so many more in the Bible. Now what are you going to do that you know you are commanded to love others as God loves us all?

Chapter 2

We Are Nothing Without Love

"...And though I have the gift of prophecy, and understand all mysteries and all knowledge, and though I have all faith, so that I could remove mountains, but have not love, I am nothing." (I Co 13:2)

Wow! "**But to have not love, I am nothing.**" Those are chilling powerful words when you meditate on them. Read them again. I don't know about you, but I would rather have *love* more than anything, because I don't want my life to be lived in vain. All our prayer should be:

> **"Lord, give us a willing heart to learn how to love Yor more, so we can love our fellow brothers and sisters more. Lord, we don't care if we prophesy, understand all mysteries and have all knowledge and faith to remove**

mountains–just help us grow in love as You would have us to."

Of course, we need to understand there is nothing wrong with having those gifts and abilities, and we should have them, for they are helpful in building up the Kingdom of God. However, to possess those beneficial gifts and have not love in our heart for God and people is where real danger comes in. Thanks be to God, it does not matter to Him how much knowledge, understanding, faith, talents and gifts we have; but what truly does matter to Him is how much love we have for Him and our brothers and sisters. Our gifts should never out weight our love for God, for loving God first gives us the power, ability and strength to love others and share in blessing them.

We must work diligently against developing a stony heart: a hard or cold heart, a heart that does not love, a heart that does not forgive, a heart that hates and full of malice and deceit. Why? because the enemy is always working to insert as much hate, fear, confusion and negativity in our minds and hearts as he possibly can; that's his job. That's why we must be on our job too: making sure we have a soft heart of flesh by purposely keeping our Father and God at the forefront of our consciousness; by reading His Word and committing to the first commandment, which is to do what Jesus said, *"You shall love the LORD your God with all your heart, with all your soul, with all your strength, and with all your mind,' and 'your neighbor as yourself" (Luke 10:27).* You see, real love begins with knowing God and surrendering our lives to Him. See, God is Love, and He is the only One Who is able and capable of loving us on the deep level our soul's truly desire. Our spouses, children or friends can't, no matter how much they try. Only God loves us with the ultimate *Love*. And oh, what love! It's more real than anything you ever experienced in this world. Yes, God is wonderfully loving, and He is also peacefully comforting. He is the only One Who can give us that kind of love and peace, and both beautifully passes all understanding.

Now, God already knows all about you; But He desires you get to know Him, because He is *"...not willing that any should perish but that all should come to repentance." (II Peter3:9)*. Thus, each one of us have a personal responsibility to get to know our Creator and God–developing a close personal relationship with Him. This will enable us to be kind to one another, love and forgive one another, and keep His Word clean. Paul said in Ephesians 4:32, *"And be kind to one another, tenderhearted, forgiving one another, just as God in Christ forgave you."* Jesus said, *"This is My commandment, that you love one another as I have loved you" (John 15:12)*. John said, *"Beloved, let us love one another, for love is of God, and everyone who loves has been born of God, and knows God (1 John 4:7)*. The question is, are you born of God's Spirit, or the spirit of the other one? Paul said, *"Let all that you do be done with love (1 Corinthians 16:14)*. Love is an action word: it carries with it genuine feelings, concerns, compassion, care, empathy and consideration for others. You see, love is important because love

14

makes our hearts tender toward others. Peter said, *"Finally, all of you be of one mind, having compassion for one another; love as brothers, be tenderhearted, be courteous" (1 Peter 3:8).*

There is a reason the word *"love"* is recorded in the Bible way over 500 times, and the exact phrase *"love" one another* "is written over a dozen times. So, loving one another is of great priority to God; and why should it not be since He is Love Himself? God makes it plain through Paul what we need to focus on and strive for if we really profess to know and love God. Those of us who do not know God—it's time to make your choice, and choose to find out about Him, because rather you know it or not you would not be alive if it was not for God keeping you. I am sure none of us want to live our lives in vain, missing the mark, or missing out on the most important thing in the world that our Lord and God wants us to do the most. Love! Why? because *love does no harm to no man; therefore, love is the fulfillment of the law (Romans 13:10).*

God taught me about the importance of love when He first came into my life in 1995. He asked me a question early one morning soon as I had awakened. He asked, ***"Do you want to know the secret of the universe?"*** I was shocked He asked that question and was very hesitant to answer, because I was afraid His response would be too profound for my little pea mind to comprehend. So, I waited a good while before I braced myself and answered, yes Lord, I want to know! Then He simply said, ***"It's Love."*** I then breathed deeply with a sigh of relief and said,

"Is that all!" There I was thinking He was going to blow my mind with a profound answer about the Solar System or something. At that time, I did not realize He wanted to teach me the depth and power of love and how extremely important *Love* truly is. He wanted me to know that *Love* is the heart of the matter–*Love* is the substance or main ingredient; it is the core factor or element in life. In other words, Love is vitally crucial or essentially critical for living a healthy whole joyful life;

God also wanted to teach me, that not only is He Love, but He is the founding source of Love. He told me these very words just as they are written here. He said, ***"Source is where all things originate from. I am the Source of all things. Love is deep, deep in your soul where all meaning for life is formed. You are formed out of deep love.*** I thought, wow! So, our God and Heavenly Father is the Source of all things: He is the Source of Love, or the Central or Dominant Chief of Love; He is the Foundation or Ultimate of Love. Can you see why it's so essentially critical to our God and Heavenly Father that His children Love one another!

There was another time when God asked me about *Love*. On morning while I was on my knees praying, He asked me out of the clear blue, ***"Do you love food more than Me?"*** I was more shocked at that question than the first one. It never crossed my mind that God would have the slightest interested in what I ate; let alone ask me about it. I think the question surprised me more than anything. You see I really loved and enjoyed eating my food, it always tasted so good—delicious is a better word, especially for my deserts. I was like a happy little kid whenever I was eating food—Meanwhile, I honestly started to cry while thinking about how to answer Him, because I wanted to be totally honest. So, after about two or three minutes of serious thinking, I finally answered and said, "No Lord, I don't love food more than You, because if it were not for You I would not be able to enjoy my food so much."

I learned God desires we love Him more than anything or anyone else. He has that right. He created us. We are His. That's why the first commandment is the greatest, that we love Him *with all our heart, with all our soul, with all our strength, and with all our mind, and our neighbor as ourselves, (Luke 10:27)* After all, God is *a jealous God*, and I am glad He is. He wants us to put Him first, because when we put Him first in our lives–we have a better life: A more peaceful and fulfill life. His ways, if followed, keeps us out of trouble and stop us from hurting others. God spoke these words to Moses for the children of Israel; they are just as relevant for us today as they were then. He said, *"'I am the LORD your God who brought you out of the land of Egypt, out of the house of bondage. 'You shall have no other gods before Me. You shall not bow down to them nor serve them. For I, the LORD your God, am a jealous God, ..."* (Deuteronomy 5:6-7, 9). I understand today, that without loving Him first, it would be difficult to love others as we should. Since God is Love, then He is the secret of the universe, and He definitely makes the world go round.

God has created, established and is the sustainer of the whole cosmos, including the earth. God said, *"I have made the earth, and created man upon it: I, even my hands, have stretched out the heavens, and all their host have I commanded" (Isaiah 45:12).* Truly if our God and Father wasn't the Loving, Gracious, Merciful, Forgiving Sovereign Creator, Orchestrator and Regulator of the universe where would any of us be? God has truly created and is holding the entire world in His hand. I already listed some scriptures above in the introduction on how great God is, but listen to a few more on the power of God and What He has done below:

"Thus says God the LORD, Who created the heavens and stretched them out, Who spread forth the earth and that which comes from it, Who gives breath to the people on it, And spirit to those who walk on it, (Isaiah 42:5). Can you see from this scripture that God gave you your breath and put His Spirit in you? If not, listen to the powerful words the anointed apostle Paul spoke, *"God, who made the world and everything in it, since He is Lord of heaven and earth, does not dwell in temples made with hands. Nor is He worshiped with men's hands, as though He needed anything, since He gives to all life, breath, and all things. And He has made from one blood every nation of men to dwell on all the face of the earth, and has determined their preappointed times and the boundaries of their dwellings, so that they*

should seek the Lord, in the hope that they might grope for Him and find Him, though He is not far from each one of us; for in Him we live and move and have our being, as also some of your own poets have said, 'For we are also His offspring," (Acts 17:24-28).

Truly, we are His offspring. Truly our God is the Source of everyone and everything? Truly, Love is the Master, and the Master holds the key, for the key is Love and the Master surely Rules from heaven above with WISDOM POWER AND LOVE; so much so that we don't fully understand it. The Prophet Jeremiah said,

"He has made the earth by His power, He has established the world by His wisdom, And has stretched out the heavens at His discretion" (Jeremiah 10:12). I can't leave out what the Prophet Isaiah said, *"Have you not known? Have you not heard? Has it not been told you from the beginning? Have you not understood from the foundations of the earth? It is He who sits above the circle of the earth, And its inhabitants are like grasshoppers, Who stretches out the heavens like a curtain, And spreads them out like a tent to dwell in"* *(Isaiah 40:21-22).*

Listen further to the power of our God. *"He brings the princes to nothing; He makes the judges of the earth useless. Scarcely shall they be planted, Scarcely shall they be sown, Scarcely shall their stock take root in the earth, When He will also blow on them, And they will wither, And the whirlwind will take them away like stubble. To whom then will you liken Me, Or to whom shall I be equal?" says the Holy One.* *"Have you not known? Have you not heard? The everlasting God, the LORD, The Creator of the ends of the earth, Neither faints nor is weary. His understanding is unsearchable."* *(Isaiah 40:23-25, Isaiah 40:28).* The Apostle Paul says, *"Oh, the depth of the riches both of the wisdom and knowledge of God! How unsearchable are His judgments and His ways past finding out!" (Romans 11:33).*

How great and awesome is our God? Greater than all that is! He is so great that it really ought to make us feel humble. Clearly God has created the earth and sent us here on it with His breath and Spirit inside us. What God said to our forefather's yesteryear, God is saying the same thing to us today through His Word, because God is the same yesterday, today and forever. He doesn't change (Hebrews13:8). If we can understand what a Mighty God we serve, it may help us have more faith in Him. Isaiah said, *"Thus says the LORD, your Redeemer, And He who formed you from the womb: "I am the LORD, who makes all things, Who stretches out the heavens all alone, Who spreads abroad the earth by Myself" (Isaiah 44:24).* The reason I quoted these many scriptures is so you could really understand that God has created the world, and us, and if He created the world and us, shouldn't He know Who and What makes the world go round? He said it is LOVE!

Now if you do not know God, the first thing you must do is get to know your Creator and God and learn how to love Him with all your heart, with all your soul, with all your strength and with all your mind, and your neighbor as yourself, Luke 10:27. He has created you to get to know Him as your Creator. He wants you to know how much He love you too. He wants you to learn to love as He desires you to love. If you never get to know your Creator, you will never know how much He loves you; you will never know how much He want you to love others, and you will never know how much you can love. You will never know how it feels to be loved by the ONE Who created you! Please don't miss out on His love. It's the best thing that can ever happen to you.

Therefore, the 13th Chapter of first Corinthians is reminding us that all our achievements, talents, accumulations and gifts are nothing without love. We are foolish to think we are solely responsible for any of our own successes without recognizing God is behind it all, because all we have and all we are, comes from almighty God, through us, not from us. He is the Source of everything. Therefore, let's all practice letting love lead us to *"Love"* becoming more like our God and Father.

We need to let our motives and deeds be rooted and grounded in Love—in Him. We need to be careful that we don't set ourselves up as superior to others. We need to understand that our Heavenly Father truly loves us deeply and unconditionally; He wants His children to be the image or reflection of His love, and help spread love around. But more importantly, we need to remember not only does He love us unconditionally, but He sees everything we do, and He knows everything about us.

Listen to what God is saying to us. *"But let him who glories glory in this, That he understands and knows Me, That I am the LORD, exercising lovingkindness, judgment, and righteousness in the earth. For in these I delight," says the LORD"* (Jeremiah 9:24). *"For his eyes are upon the ways of man, and he sees all his steps* (Job 34:21). *"The eyes of the LORD are in every place, beholding the evil and the good"* (Proverbs 15:3). *"The LORD looked down from heaven upon the children of men, to see if there were any that did understand, and seek God"* (Psalms 14:2). And Psalms 139:3 says this, *"You comprehend my path and my lying down, And are acquainted with all my ways."*

Clearly, we see from God's Word that He loves us and He knows all about us. He knows all about me, you and everyone else. Job says He sees all our ways. *"Does He not see my ways, And count all my steps? If I have walked with falsehood, Or if my foot has hastened to deceit..."* (Job 31:3-4). Now, listen to what David said, *"You know my sitting down and my rising up; You understand my thought afar off. You comprehend my path and my lying down, And are acquainted with all my ways. For there is not a word on my tongue, But behold, O LORD, You know it* altogether" *(Psalms 139:2-4).* Now that's the knowledge and power of the Loving God we serve! So, our God is absolutely aware of us all the time. You might not feel it, and you might not know it, you might not believe it, but you are always in God's presence, and one day we all must give an account to our God for how we have lived our lives. Are you living a life of love?

God is Love, God is real. God's Word is alive. Listen to the power, aliveness and realness of God's Word. *"For the Word of God is living and powerful, and sharper than any two-edged sword, piercing even to the division of soul and spirit, and of joints and marrow, and is a discerner of the thoughts and intents of the heart. And there is no creature hidden from His sight, but all things are naked and open to the eyes of Him to whom we must give account" (Heb 4:12-13).* Please take the time to get to know your Creator and God while you still have time, before it's too late! Because you are going to die one day and you are going to meet "Love/God" and He is going to ask you two questions, how have you loved, and why haven't you forgiven your brother or sister?

Chapter 3

Genuine Love Profits Much

"...And though I bestow all my goods to feed the poor, and though I give my body to be burned, but have not love, it profits me nothing." (I Co 13:3)

Do you know that love is only profitable when it is passed around? Do you know that however you treat others, you will be treated the same way? Whatever we give out, is what we will get back. That being said, let's begin acting how we want to be treated; giving out what we want to get back, for what we sow, that we shall also reap. The Bible says, *"Be not deceived; God is not mocked: for whatsoever a man soweth, that shall he also reap" (Galatians 6:7).*

Since God is not mocked, and since we will reap what we sow, we need to do those things that's not deceiving, but those

25

things that are profitable and do them with love. We must learn to let love be our motivation behind our actions. We cannot fool God and no use trying. He knows what's in our hearts better than we know what's in our own hearts. He said, *"The heart is deceitful above all things, And desperately wicked; Who can know it? I the LORD search the heart and test the mind, to give every man according to his ways, according to the fruit of his deeds"* *(Jeremiah 17:9-10)*. *"And now abide faith, hope, love, these three; but the greatest of these is love (1 Corinthians 13:13)*. So, love is the most important element of all in God's eyes. Love is the first fruit of the spirit. That's why Jesus gave us a new commandment: *"A new commandment I give to you, that you love one another; as I have loved you, that you also love one another"* *(John 13:34)*.

Of course, there is nothing wrong with you giving all your goods to feed the poor, or even giving your body to be burned, if that's what you choose to do, but I don't think I could do that, but feed the poor, yes. We are supposed to help others, especially the poor; but to do it without love in your heart will profit you nothing in the eyes of God. However, if genuine love is in our hearts and love is our motive, then we are doing what our Heavenly Father want us to do; and He is pleased with us. Our deeds will profit others and us good returns and our souls will also prosper spiritually. God wants us to prosper both physically and spiritually. John said, *"Beloved, I wish above all things that thou mayest prosper and be in health, even as thy soul prospers"*

(3 John 2). We want a healthy inner spirit as well as a healthy outer physical body.

God give us according to the fruit of our deeds. He tells us how to sow or give, and what should be out attitude when giving. In II Corinthians 9:6-7 it says, *"But this I say, He which soweth sparingly shall reap also sparingly; and he which soweth bountifully shall reap also bountifully. Every man according as he purposed in his heart, so let him give; not grudgingly, or of necessity: for God loveth a cheerful giver."* Then in Luke 6:38 He says, *"Give, and it will be given to you: good measure, pressed down, shaken together, and running over will be put into your bosom. For with the same measure that you use, it will be measured back to you."* God is saying to us through these scriptures, we can't out give Him. So go ahead, and be a giving, kind and freehearted person, because *"The liberal soul shall be made fat: and he those waters shall be watered also himself"* *(Proverbs 11:25).*

Love must be our main focus if we want to please our God and have peace in our hearts. We do not want to do what we do to be seen by others or to impress them. We do not want to seek praise and recognition from men, but do what we do to the glory and honor of our God. We want to give to and serve others with a pure heart and a sincere conscious for those we are doing it for. We purify our souls and hearts when we give—obeying God's Words of truth. Thus, Peter encourages us to be honest and truthful when it comes to loving our brothers and sisters in Christ with these words. *"Since you have purified your souls in obeying the truth through the Spirit in sincere love of the brethren, love one another fervently with a pure heart"* (1 Peter 1:22). So having a pure heart and being honest in what we do is also very much the key.

God encourages us to be righteous, for He says in Hosea 10:12, *"Sow for yourselves righteousness; Reap in mercy; Break up your fallow ground, For it is time to seek the LORD, Till He comes and rains righteousness on you."* Thus, we need to sow good seeds and do good deeds of the best kind in support of others that we may receive mercy and also give mercy. We need to make sure our hearts do not become unfeeling and unsympathetic by reaching out more to comfort, strengthen and encourage others. More importantly, we need to keep our minds rooted and renewed in the Word of God that He will reward our righteousness.

It is to our profit that we sow righteousness through loving and helping others. For God words says, *"He who sows iniquity will reap sorrow, And the rod of his anger will fail. He who has a generous eye will be blessed, For he gives of his bread to the poor"* (Proverbs 22:8-9). In other words, the person who sows wickedly will have sorrow and heap up shame and trouble on himself; the person who sows good and shows mercy to others will reap generous blessings upon his soul. The Word says, *"The merciful man does good for his own soul, But he who is cruel troubles his own flesh (Proverbs 11:17).* Wow, it's good to be good and show mercy than be cruel and wicked; isn't it? I don't think any of us want to trouble our own flesh by acting foolishly and wickedly for the Word says, *"The wicked man does deceptive work, But he who sows' righteousness will have a sure reward (Proverbs 11:18)."* Amen*!*

Having a sure reward is being unquestionably certain that we will gain the gracious blessings of God. When we have a soul that loves with a deep feeling of passion and compassion, we love each other like our Heavenly Father loves us all. When we honestly love and care we are more prone to help others. Someone said, "One soul is worth more than the whole world." I believe that because of what Jesus said about one person repenting, *"I say to you that likewise there will be more joy in heaven over one sinner who repents than over ninety-nine just persons who need no repentance,"* *(Luke 15:7).* Not only will there be joy in heaven when one person repents, but likewise, *"... there is joy in the presence of the angels of God over one sinner who repents,"* *(Luke 17;10).* So, repenting of your wrong is the beginning of saving your soul, and getting right with God.

Child of God, do you have soul–not a soul? Do you have passion, depth, thirst, hunger and a desire to help others? Whoever you are, do you really have soul? Do you have that deep hardcore essence to sincerely love others as yourself? I admit some people may be hard to love, but we should practice loving them too, for It is easy to love those who love us, but God want us to go out of our circle and love others. Of course, there are some who do not love themselves as they should, but God wants us to love ourselves too. I believe God loving us so much is what gives us the ability to truly love others. Are we going to be soul-winning-soldiers in God's army, or are we going to sit in the comfort of our dwellings waiting for someone else to demonstrate God's love? Remember, *love* is an action word, and there are many lost souls out there yearning, seeking and starving for God's love, but they don't know it's His love they seek and starve for. Let's pray God help us be their answer to show them His love through us.

Let's lose our life so we can truly find our real life in Christ Jesus, for truly our identity is found in the life of Jesus. He said, "*...I am the way, the truth, and the life...*" *(John 14:6)*. Let's save more than our own souls by fervently venturing out and showing others God's love, soothing their starving souls. Jesus said in Mark 8:35-38 *"For whoever desires to save his life will lose it, but whoever loses his life for My sake and the gospel's will save it. For what will it profit a man if he gains the whole world, and loses his own soul? Or what will a man give in exchange for his soul?*

You do not have enough money to buy your own soul; I don't care if you are a Billionaire, or Trillionaire, your soul can't be bought, for it belongs to God, the Creator and Controller of the universe! There is no amount of money, gold or silver that we can pay for our own soul; and neither can we save our own soul, but God can. Our soul, essence or, lifeforce doesn't belong to us, but to God, the One Who gave it. Paul said, *"For you are bought with a price: therefore, glorify God in your body, and in your spirit, which are God's (1 Corinthians 6:20)*. Jesus purchased us out of love with His precious blood when He died on the cross for our sins. (Eph 1:14, 1 Pe 1:19). God sent Jesus to save the whole world; not condemn it, but to save all mankind. Man, only need to accept what Jesus has done for him; and accept Him as his Lord and Savior to be saved from bondage and hell.

That is how valuable our souls are to God. That is why Jesus has commanded us to love and care enough about one another to help save their soul. It's our duty as God's children to share God's love with others and be not ashamed on His return. He said, *"For whoever is ashamed of Me and My words in this adulterous and sinful generation, of him the Son of Man also will be ashamed when He comes in the glory of His Father with the holy angels."* So, let us be found standing strong in love for Christ' sake and the gospel' sake when He return.

It is to our greatest profit that we choose to love God and others because He first loved us. Many need to lose their frail, feeble unhappy, unpeaceful, sad sinful lifestyles—to gain the lifestyle more abundantly that Christ came to give us; which is a life of redemption, beauty, grace, mercy, peace, love, joy and forgiveness. God did not want puppets or robots is why He gave us freedom to choose. If we do not choose to love God and others by taking hold of the abundant life in Christ, Satan will continue to make our lives miserable with all sorts of negativity: like fear, confusion, deceit, dread, suffering, jealousy, bitterness, trouble, hopelessness, worry, strife, anxiety, disorder, despair, hurt, hatred, pain, depression, anguish, and any other negative and harmful feeling. He will muddle up our lives any way he can. So, watch out!

We must remember that Satan is not only the destroyer; he is the deceiver, he is the disruptor, he is the divider of God's people and the demolisher of all that is good. Jesus called him Satan the devil, a murderer, a liar, no truth is in him, and he is the father of lies (John 8:44). Jesus said, *"The thief does not come except to steal, and to kill, and to destroy."* But He said, *I have come that they may have life, and that they may have it more abundantly" (John 10:10).*

So, let's not allow Satan to rob us of the abundant life that Jesus came to give us by dying on that cross for us. He did it of His own free will—because God loved us so. God didn't make Him do it, and no man took his life from Him by force, against His will, or before the right time. Jesus said, *"No one takes it (His life) from Me, but I lay it down of Myself. I have power to lay it down, and I have power to take it again. This command I have received from My Father" (John 10:18).* That's why Jesus rose again on the third day, because He had the power from His Father to do so. Now, He is seated at the right hand of God waiting to return again. Let's be found ready, working, watching, waiting and praying! For greater love has no man than what Jesus did, He laid down His life for us!

Chapter 4

Love Does Not Boast

"...Love suffers long and is kind; love does not envy; love does not parade itself, is not puffed up" (I Co 13:4)

Most of us get a little impatient at times, but how would you like being around annoyed, irritated or edgy people all the time; intolerant of everyone and everything? At the same time, many feel somewhat prideful and a little superior to others. Well, love does not feel that way. Love is patient, longsuffering and kind. Love doesn't display itself through ego, pride, haughtiness and conceit. Neither is love envious, jealous, covetous or arrogant, and love is certainly not thinking more highly of yourself than you ought; for you are not better or more important than another. Real and tangible love causes us become unselfish, generous, noble, decent, kind, humble, and upright. Real love feels, cares, and is happy for others, for real love has no high opinion of itself. As children of God, Paul begs us to, *"Walk worthy of our calling, with all lowliness and meekness, with longsuffering, forbearing one another in love…" (Ephesians 4:2-3)*.

Paul knew and understood the problems among God's children. He also understood how important it is for love to abound, thrive and flourish among people. That's why he said walk worthy, in meekness and lowliness, longsuffering with one another in love. For love doesn't seek to be first, instead, real love, tangible love put others first, because love is the greatest human quality of all, and love is the major attribute of God Himself because He is Love!

Paul says again in Galatians 5:26 *"Let us not become conceited, provoking one another, envying one another."* And he goes on to say in another place, *"Let nothing be done through selfish ambition or conceit, but in lowliness of mind let each esteem others better than himself. Let each of you look out not only for his own interests, but also for the interests of others"* (*Philippians 2:3-4*). Then again Paul said, *"And be kind to one another, tenderhearted, forgiving one another, just as God in Christ forgave you"* (*Ephesians 4:32*).

Thank God for loving us and forgiving us even when we were still lost and messed up ourselves in sin and bondage. If God can look beyond all our faults, flaws and failures and see our needs, then we certainly had better mature up, and learn to love and forgive our brothers and sisters, because we are no better than they are. And guess what? God still love them too just as much as

He love you and me. And guess what else, many of us have even been where they are. So let us not continue to judge and condemn others any longer, but learn to love more; and thank God He is God and not us!

Peter said, *"Finally, all of you be of one mind, having compassion for one another; love as brothers, be tenderhearted, be courteous; not returning evil for evil or reviling for reviling, but on the contrary blessing, knowing that you were called to this, that you may inherit a blessing (1 Peter 3:8).* We do not need to go around getting even with anyone; and neither do we need to be insulting, rude, condemning or abusive to others; that is not love, and that is not how we as God children should behave.

Paul expressed throughout his writing how we should treat each other, saying, *"Therefore, as the elect of God, holy and beloved, put-on tender mercies, kindness, humility, meekness, longsuffering; bearing with one another, and forgiving one another, if anyone has a complaint against another; even as Christ forgave you, so you also must do. But above all these things put on love, <u>which is the bond of perfection</u>. And let the peace of God rule in your hearts, to which also you were called in one body; and be thankful" (Colossians 3:12-15).*

Can you see now how very important it is for us to learn how to forgive one another and walk-in Love. When we walk in love, we are able to get along better with everyone. Because <u>Love</u> is the master key that opens the heart; and love is the key to everything else. Peter said, *"And above all things have fervent love for one another, for "love will cover a multitude of sins. Be hospitable to one another without grumbling"* (1 Peter 4:8-9). And in the book of Proverbs it says, *"Hatred stirs up strife, But love covers all sins..."* (Proverbs 10:12). In other words, hatred seeks to provoke hostility and delight in brawls; whereas love on the other hand is patient and suffers long and seeks to overlook offences and faults of others more readily. The more of God's Word we have in us the better able we are to deal with others and their situations. Paul said again, *"Let the word of Christ dwell in you richly in all wisdom, teaching and admonishing one another in psalms and hymns and spiritual songs, ... And whatever you do in word or deed, do all in the name of the Lord Jesus, giving thanks to God* for all the grace and mercy we receive by Jesus Christ*" Colossians 3:16.-17).*

Now let's get a better understanding of what the <u>Bond of Perfection</u> is. What is the Bond of Perfection? (1) The Bond of Perfection is the thing which will unite all other things, making them whole and complete. (2) The Bond of Perfection completes and keeps things together. (3) The Bond of Perfection gathers together the rest, which, without it, would be loose and disconnected. (4) The Bond of Perfection is binding together all the other graces into one whole, making the child of God feel fulfilled. Simply put—The Bond of Perfection is, <u>The Tie that Binds.</u> In other words, The Bond of Perfection is like a girdle, or a band or belt that holds all the various parts of everything else together. Glory Hallelujah, all praises be to the Living God! He is truly the BOND OF PERFECTION! He absolutely whole this world together by His Word, His Power, and His Spirit and His Love.

I believe the best summary for 'The Bond of Perfection is to say, it's like a magnet, pulling and drawing all things and everyone to itself; holding it <u>All</u> together by the power of unconditional perfect love. It's as though God has loved us with all of Himself: Now we are to love Him with all of ourselves. That's why Jesus said what He said, *"You shall love the LORD your God with all your heart, with all your soul, with all your strength, and with all your mind,' and 'your neighbor as yourself"* *(Luke 10:27)*. When we live that verse, we are doing just that— loving God with all our being. I can see clearly how LOVE, OR GOD pulls and holds all else together—making all things complete and whole. Can you see it?

Do you know that God loves us not because of what we do, or that we are that good, but because He is so Good! God loves us because He doesn't know spite, vindictiveness, envy, greed, jealousy or resentment. God loves us because He is not big-headed, puffed up or egotistical–because He is God. God doesn't love us because He is Almighty, Prevailing and Powerful; and neither does He love us because He has the authority to command us to love others. God loves us simply because He is Love and His Nature and Character is Love. It is by God's love to us, and our love to others that love is to be maintained, preserved and passed on. Love begets love. The more a man loves God, the more he is enabled to love his neighbor, and the more he is enabled and empowered to love his neighbor the more love is spread around; the more love is spread around, the better the world go round. So, let's all get on board with our Heavenly Father and start loving others more, because He has commanded us to, and because He loved us first, deeply and unconditionally. No strings attached, except believe, trust and obey Him.

We know God's love is not selfish because it is impossible for God to be selfish. He is unlimited, unrestricted, unrestrained, uninhibited, uncontrolled and He is totally unselfish. *For He so loved the world, that He gave His only begotten Son* to die for our sins to redeem us back to Himself. If that's not love–what is? He supplies all our needs in abundance. He gives sweet peace to our troubling minds, He give us joy in our spirit, He comforts our yearning souls, and He forgives us every time we faulter. He wants us to forgive others as He forgives us. He wants His children to become more and more like Him: forgiving others seventy times seven, until we become selfless. Listen to how Jesus' answered Peter, *"Then Peter came to Him and said, "Lord, how often shall my brother sin against me, and I forgive him? Up to seven times? Jesus said to him, I do not say to you, up to seven times, but up to seventy times seven" (Matthew 18:21-22)*.

God, Who is love, and those who love as God loves—absolutely make the world go round. Not only does God/Love make the world go round—He is holding it together and everything else in it securely in place with the <u>Bond of Perfection</u>;

which, is His Great, Endless, immeasurable, Vast, Infinite and Unconditional Love. So, Love is the Master Key that binds God's heart to man, and man's heart to other men hearts. Love opens the door of the heart, and love is the key to true happiness and abundant life; and love is walking in the purpose of God; living well, loving much and laughing often: more importantly, obeying the Word of the Lord our God. Someone said, "We have only one life that will soon pass, only what's done for Christ will last."

Chapter 5

Love Seeks Not Its Own

"...Love does not behave rudely, does not seek its own, is not provoked, thinks no evil." (I Co 13:5).

Did you ever wonder why you were too easy going and always willing to help others? Did you ever wonder why you couldn't do some of the mischievous things your friends did? Could it be because you were concerned more about others than yourself, but you didn't know it? Love is a strange thing, because love will keep you from doing mischievous things you may want to do, but cannot, while your friends did mischievous things with no problem. Did you ever think why you couldn't do what others did was because love wouldn't let you do wrong mischievous hurtful things to others. Loves cares and love protects us and others. Thank God, He created us with an innate discernment, and gave us His Word to direct our path.

Love is a strange thing because love will tolerate wrong like it tolerates right. Did you know that God make the sun rise on the evil and on the good alike? Did you know that God sends rain on the just and on the unjust alike? The Bible says, *"... for He makes His sun to rise on the evil and on the good, and sends rain on the just and on the unjust"* (Matthew 5:45). Did you know God sent His Son to die for the righteous and the unrighteous alike? Of Jesus, John said, *"And he is the propitiation for our sins: and not for ours only, but also for the sins of the whole world" (1 John 2:2).* You see, Jesus was righteous, but He came and took the punishment for the sins of the unrighteous as well as the righteous. He suffered, bled and died, rose from the dead reconciling us to our Father and God. Jesus did not die for the sins of a select group of people, but for all mankind. Thank You LORD!

Now, why would the Almighty Righteous, Just and Holy God send His righteous and Holy Son to die for a world of messed-up sinners such as you and I? The Bible says, *for God so loved the world*–to such a great extent–*that He sent His only begotten Son,* that He may save all His others sons and daughters, you and I, from a life of sin and bondage and eternal damnation. Again, thank You Lord for loving us so!

Our God and Heavenly Father really loves us unconditionally with an everlasting love. He is always drawing us to Himself because of His deep unconditional love for us. Listen to what Jeremiah said, *"The LORD has appeared of old to me, saying: "Yes, I have loved you with an everlasting love;*

Therefore, with lovingkindness I have drawn you" (Jeremiah 31:3). Not only does God love us with an everlasting love, He always wants the very best for us: to give us peace, hope and a good future. God spoke these words to Jeremiah in times past, they still apply to us today. He said, *"For I know the thoughts that I think toward you, says the LORD, thoughts of peace and not of evil, to give you a future and a hope" (Jeremiah 29:11).*

Just as God's thoughts of us are good and not evil, so also our thoughts towards others should be good and not evil. Love thinks highly of a person' best qualities, not on their flaws, mistakes or shortcoming. We should not intentionally provoke fights, arouse unnecessary feelings of anger in others. Love strives to have the other person best interests at heart, because love considers others before itself. God wants us to love people well by treating them well.

If someone is feeling discouraged, or depressed, love will try to encourage or bring joy by uplifting them, not tear them down. Love endures hardship with patience and understanding, not that it will be easy, and sometime requires much prayer. Love also has feeling and compassion for others. Love simply loves and just want to help, because love is an action word and that is what love does. Those who love sees and seeks to fulfill the needs of others—many times before their own needs are met. Love will show grace and mercy, instead of judgement and punishment. That sounds like what God did for us when He sent His only begotten Son to die for our sins—doesn't it? He didn't send Jesus

44

to condemn and judge us, but to save us through grace and truth. Thank God for His grace and mercy toward us.

It's important to God that we *"love"* one another as He has commanded us to. We all need to grow and mature in God and love toward one another—learning to exercise being kind, caring, unselfish, gentle, moral, good, patient, thoughtful and considerate toward each other more. We need to learn how to show feelings of concern and empathy for our fellow brothers and sisters.

For God has certainly shown love, goodness, kindness, grace and forgiveness to all of us and we don't deserve it. Now, God expects us to spread His goodness—spreading Him around; for He is Love! *"love"* is the greatest of all the fruit of the spirit; for love covers a multitude of sin and love never, never fails, because God never fails. The Love of God truly does make the world go round, because He is the Tie that Binds us and the world to Himself! Without Him there would be no world, or us! We didn't just happen to pop up one day as some may believe! We were created by the Creator, God!

When we honestly know that our God loves us unconditionally, we are freer to love others. This is why Paul laid out the power of love so beautifully in I Corinthians the 13th Chapter. And he goes on to tell us in 1 Corinthians 10:24 saying, *"Let no one seek his own, but each one the other's well -being."* And in Philippians 2:4 Paul said, *"Look not every man on his own things, but every man also on the things of others:* And John said, *"Beloved, let us love one another, for love is of God, and everyone who loves has been born of God, and knows God (1 John 4:7).* Amen! If you don't know that you have been born or the Spirit of God–ask yourself whose spirit, are you born of? Many times, one can tell which Spirit others are born of by their fruit; their love for others, their behavior, character or mannerism.

For those of you who love others deeply, it is because you have been born of God, and you know God. John says further, *"Everyone who has been born of God does not commit sin, because His seed remains in him, and he cannot sin, because he has been born of God" (1 John 3:9).* Meaning, your nature, outlook, viewpoint or thinking has been transformed, or born of the Spirit of God. Is your mind still conformed to the mind-set of this dark, sinful present world, or has it been born of God? In other words, has your mind been renewed with the Word of our God?

I am recalling something pertaining to this subject I wrote in my book, *Joy and Gladness* a few years back. I would like to share it with you here. God awaken me from a very pleasant, but unusual dream around 6:00 am on a Thursday morning in September of 2009. The details of the dream were many and vivid, but I will not go into all the details except the ones mentioned here. In the dream, three people out of a room full of people who were all busy doing some kind of work; or conversing with each other—they gathered around me and gently escorted me through what seems as a big industrial kitchen–on to a big tall silver heavy door. They opened it, and slightly helped me outside this door. It immediately shut behind me. The second it did I was instantly aware that I could not turn and go back inside. I knew I had to proceed ahead, as I heard God say the words, *"This is what will happen when you can't come back through this door."*

I assumed that maybe I had died and was going to meet my deeds. I was not afraid, but curious and surprised at what happened. Immediately, five very warm, friendly, courteous, and polite young men came to meet me. They greeted me graciously and were eager and willing to assist me. Suddenly, what looked as a car pulled up in front of us. They all were ready and willing to help me get into this vehicle by opening the door and gesturing with their hands out toward me as they bowed their heads and said welcoming words, but I cannot remember what the words were.

It seems their main goal was to escort or assist me, making me very comfortable and well pleased, and making sure I got to where I was going. They closed the doors to this vehicle, and we talked a lot as they drove but I do not remember what we talked about. They drove me to two different building. At the first building this lady behind the podium was speaking to the audience about doing more for God without making excuses–by using the word, "But." I realized that people needed to choose; making up their minds who they will serve.

The second building we visited, this man behind the podium was proclaiming the word of God strongly. His voice was profound, soulful and heart touching, and he was extremely sincere as he spoke. The words *"Hear what God has to say."* seemed to come from deep within his being in a singing tone. I noticed he held each word for a length of time. I also noticed; I was listening very intently to what he was saying. Those six words stuck in my head, *"Hear what God has to say."*.

Between the two stops these young men escorted me in and out of this vehicle that was similar to a car, and in and out of each building we stopped at. The kindness, politeness and courtesy of these five young men continued to be unbelievable warm, friendly, and well-mannered, as they made sure I was pleased, comfortable and satisfied. I could not help but notice each of them because they were extraordinary kind to me. Their faces were unfamiliar. I let them know that I appreciated their kindness toward me. They all had very neat and trimmed haircuts and were dressed in clean normal plain clothes. As I looked intently at each of them, I noticed two were young teenagers, the other three were mature and older looking young men. I was so amazed at the hospitality they were showing toward me; I just stood and stared trying to figure out why they were so kind? I did not feel like I deserved it.

As they drove me from the first destination to the second destination, I retained these words in my spirit, *Praise God More! Praise God More, Praise God more!* Then I could feel myself being drawn or pulled away very slowly, as God was awakening me. When I awakened, I could hear these words as they rang loud in my ears and spirit, *"Hear what God has to say. Hear what God has to say."* I opened my eyes and lie there in bed as I continued repeating those six words. I then got up and went right to my computer and this is what I heard the Father say as I began to type:

"Hear Me child, I love you all who love Me and do My Will and not your own thing; and just as I have loved you, love everybody else. I have more love waiting for you on the other side of the door. The door will surely close. Death will take you to another door---the door of life eternal where you will spend it with Me throughout all eternity, so love well! Hear Me when I say, I'll have peace, love, joy, happiness, and good will for all who come to Me. So, make room inside your heart for more of Me." I realized God was showing me how much He loved me through the amazing kindness of those five young hospitable men.

That is just one of the messages He gave me to share. As you see, it is all about us loving one another well as He loves us all. When I first started writing books He said to me, **"Write down what I tell you. You must write your way to people who need you."** That is what I have done in the other seven preceding books. He loves to share more of Himself with us as we get closer to Him.

After I finished writing and publishing the seventh book in

January of 2020; I was done–through with writing books! So, I thought. The number seven represented completion for me. However, one morning after I finished reading a chapter on, *Choosing A Blessed/Happy Life* from my book, *Joy And gladness,* I was suddenly filled with joy and a strong desire to write another book, and title it, *Choosing the Happy Life.* But as I lie in bed, I thought, NO! That's not the right title. A few minutes later—out of the blue, I heard the Holy Spirit say, *"Love Makes the World Go Round,"* I knew right away God had given me the title of what He wanted me to write about as well as the desire and inspiration to write. Thus, I guess I was not done after all. I remembered He did tell me once when I was about to embark on *Invisible Shield,* when I thought I could not write it, because I thought I had said everything I had to say in the first book, *White Light.* He said to me, **"I have to keep my children busy."** It looks like He has done just that. God keeps His Word!

He said that the door of death would surely close one day and another door would open. He told me to make room inside my heart for more of Him. All the Father wants is for all His children to make more room in their hearts for more of Him. Forgiving one another more, loving one another more, showing kindness to one another more. He has promised us that more will be waiting for us on the other side of death's door.

Look, see how much love God has already shown us. ***"For God so loved the world that He gave His only begotten Son, that whoever believes in Him should not perish but have*** *everlasting life," John 3:16.*

"For when we were still without strength, in due time Christ died for the ungodly. For scarcely for a righteous man will one die; yet perhaps for a good man someone would even dare to die. But God demonstrates His own love toward us, in that while we were still sinners, Christ died for us" (Romans 5:6-7).

"By this we know love, because He laid down His life for us. And we also ought to lay down our lives for the brethren," (1 John 3:16). Lord, help us all to surely learn how to love well!

"In this is love, not that we loved God, but that He loved us and sent His Son to be the propitiation for our sins" (I John 4:10).

"Jesus answered and said to him, "If anyone loves Me, he will keep My word; and My Father will love him, and We will come to him and make Our home with him (John 14:23). They absolutely come! If you don't believe it, try them and see!

"If someone says, "I love God," and hates his brother, he is a liar; for he who does not love his brother whom he has seen, how can he love God whom he has not seen? And this commandment we have from Him: that he who loves God must love his brother also" (1 John 4:20-21).

Jesus showed us the greatest love of all. *"Greater love has no one than this, than to lay down one's life for his friends.*

51

(John 15:13) Why did God send Jesus to do something so incredibly extreme and wonderfully amazing for us—who are not even worthy? Because *"God desires all men to be saved and come to the knowledge of truth"* (I Timothy 2:4). Thank You Father, for loving us so much, and that You wanted us to know You! God truly wants a personal relationship with everyone who comes to Him. That's why He is always gently drawing people to Himself in one way or another. The LORD said to Hosea, *"I drew them with gentle cords, With bands of love, And I was to them as those who take the yoke from their neck. I stooped and fed them, (Hosea 11:4).*

He is still constantly drawing the lost to Himself today through His Word, through His children, you and me, and many times through divine supernatural encounters; and with His kindness, grace, mercy and His unconditional perfect love. And boy, oh boy, does He take the yoke from our necks and feed us with His truth, as well as through the Holy Spirit who lives within us. In other words, living life God's way removes our burdens. His Word enlighten our minds. His peace comforts our souls, and His love brings joy to our hearts.

Look at what Isaiah 64:6 says about us, *"But we are all like an unclean thing, And all our righteousness are like filthy rags; We all fade as a leaf, And our iniquities, like the wind, Have taken us away."* So even we at our best are not that good, but are sinful and unworthy. So, let's just start loving each other as God has commanded. For God truly is Love. and has shown us how much He loves us*! and he who abides in love abides in God, and God in him (1 John 4:16).* Amen!

Chapter 6

Love Rejoices Not in Wrong, But in Truth

"...Does not rejoice in iniquity, but rejoices in the truth" (I Co 13:6).

People with common sense, in their right mind doesn't rejoice seeing others treated wrong: inhumanely, cruelly or cold-heartedly no matter who they are. Love takes no pleasure or delight in any kind of wickedness. Injustice, inequality, unfairness, deceitfulness, prejudice, dishonesty, corruption and other evils are so prevalence in our world today. However, most of us does rejoice in truth, justice, fairness and righteousness.

Why is it so hard for some people to just be good and treat others right? Could it be because they do not know their Creator and God? Could it be that they do not know God loves them? Could it be they desire to be loved themselves? Whatever the

reason—Jesus is the answer. However, if they do not know God–
–how can they love, or know that they are loved unconditionally?
We as children of God should be demonstrating God's love
toward them through our conduct, lifestyle, speech and character.

On the other hand, Jesus talked about the evil one, the
ruler of this world, the father of lies, and how he hates God; (John
17:15, John 14:30, John 8:44, John 7:7) known as Satan. He
blinded the eyes of many and deceived the hearts and minds of
others—making it difficult for some to come to the knowledge of
truth. Nevertheless, we must continue to allow God to make His
appeal by drawing others to Himself through us. We may not be
able to affect or move some, but we should try and reach those
whose hearts are open to Him.

The main reason why some people hate followers of Jesus,
and others find it difficult or hard to treat others right is because
of what Jesus said when He walked the earth, and the same is true
today. Listen to the following passages. Jesus said, *"If the world
hates you, you know that it hated Me before it hated you" (John
15:18). "He who hates Me hates My Father also" (John 15:23).
"For everyone practicing evil hates the light and does not come to
the light, lest his deeds should be exposed" (John 3:20). "The
world cannot hate you, but it hates Me because I testify of it that
its works are evil" (John 7:7).* So, Jesus is saying, people may
dislike or hate others because their own deeds or works are evil;
thus, they choose to live in darkness rather than come to the light
of truth; they may fear their evil works will be found out by other.

56

The apostle John said this about hate and love, *"He who says he is in the light, and hates his brother, is in darkness until now. He who loves his brother abides in the light, and there is no cause for stumbling in him. But he who hates his brother is in darkness and walks in darkness, and does not know where he is going, because the darkness has blinded his eyes" (1John 2:9-11)*. In other words, some people believe their own righteousness over God's righteousness, thus, is blinded to the truth; others can't see the error of their ways, so they can't admit the truth, thus they stay in their darkness.

So, then love doesn't rejoice in hate, but rejoices in truth; and truth rejoices in righteousness, and righteousness rejoices in justice. There is never a need for a child of God to rejoice in malicious evil, injustice, immorality or any other wrongdoings, for God is a true and just God. Truth is important to both, us as individuals and to society as a whole. Truth means that we can grow and mature, learning from our pass, correcting our mistakes. Every step we take toward valuing, respecting, appreciating truth, and attack injustice and unfairness moves us closer to understanding that <u>God is truth.</u> Jesus promise that this all-important truth will heal us and make us free: (John 8:32). Free to love others and not hate them. Truth is wonderfully powerful because GOD IS TRUTH, AS WELL AS LOVE. HE IS RIGHTEOUS, AND IS ALWAYS RIGHT!

Paul said in Romans 3:3-4 that just because some people don't believe in God do not make God without effect. Listen to his words. *"For what if some did not believe? Will their unbelief make the faithfulness of God without effect? Certainly not! Indeed, let God be true but every man a liar,"* Amen! Are you going to believe what God said in His Word, or are you going to believe the words of men in this world?

Even Jesus said in *John 14:6, "I am the way, the truth, and the life. No one comes to the Father except through Me,"* Jesus was saying He is the author and eternal revealer of truth, and the giver of all life. John said, *"He who has received His testimony has certified that God is true" (John 3:33).* In other words, whoever believe in and accept Jesus as their Lord and Savior also knows that God is true. Then again Paul said, *"For we can do nothing against the truth, but for the truth" (2 Corinthians 13:8).* Paul would not speak evil, or lie against that great system of truth, but only spoke the truth God revealed to him. We do not want to be as those Paul said are, *"Always learning and never able to come to the knowledge of the truth "(2 Timothy 3:7).*

The ruler or god of this world, Satan, has done a good job on poisoning the minds of many unenlightened minded people with hate. Many are fearful and do not even understand why they are filled with hatred. They do not understand there is a real powerful entity name Satan who is behind hate; but we must remember our Holy and Almighty God is Love, and He is even more powerful than Satan, and He never fails and always wins. Therefore, please make sure you know who is behind your, thoughts, feelings, decisions and behavior. Who, or what is driving you to do what you do?

Love does not rejoice in iniquity, but love rejoices in truth, justice and righteousness. We all are subject to get caught up in some kind of sin or wrongdoing at times. However, we must not allow our wrongdoings to turn into Iniquity, because iniquity multiplies, becoming worse. Iniquity is the inner act of willfulness against others and God. It involves the attitudes of the heart that grows into bitterness, anger, jealousy, resentment and greed. Please do not give place to the devil by allowing these negative feelings to reach the greed level. Because all the devil has come to do is *steal, kill and destroy* our very minds and lives (John 10:10). Of course, we all are tempted and feel some kind-a-way many times; and we even get angry; that's why Paul said, *"Be ye angry, and sin not: let not the sun go down upon your wrath: Neither give place to the devil (Ephesians 4:26).*

Why is greed so ugly? For greed is an intense selfish and excessive desire for more than what is needed, or it could be an uncontrolled longing for increase: such as authority, money, power, control, food, drugs, sex, partying, pleasure, popularity or material things. If we want to stay in control of our thoughts and feelings, we must be careful not to give the devil space in our minds by letting our wrongdoing escalate or intensify into iniquities, because then we are caught in the enemy's trap! For not only does love not rejoice in iniquity, but without love, and rejoicing in truth, you will live the most joyless, unhappy, unpeaceful and miserable life: not finding peace and joy anywhere!

Therefore, if and when we get caught up in wrongdoing, we need to correct ourselves Straightway! Because if we don't, God Himself may have to do it for us; and don't you think He won't! Where do you think trials and tribulations come from? God test us through various trials. Our trials cause us to hurt, suffer and rethink and cry out to God; none the less, our trials come to make us strong, patient and complete according to the Word. Peter said, *"And after you have undergone pain for a little time, the God of all grace who has given you a part in his eternal glory through Christ Jesus, will himself give you strength and support, and make you complete in every good thing"* (1 Peter 5:10 BBE version). So sometimes God chasten or discipline us through our trials because He do not want us to stay in our wrongfulness; He loves us and wants us to be stronger, learning not to do wrong, becoming free from sin. However, every trial is not from God, but many times we bring suffering and difficulty upon ourselves by making bad choices.

The Bible says, *"For whom the LORD loves He corrects, Just as a father the son in whom he delights"* (Proverbs 3:12). Then again, He says *"As many as I love, I rebuke and chasten. Therefore, be zealous and repent"* (Revelation 3:19). So not only does God chasten us as His children, but He tells us to chasten our own children. Listen, *"Chasten your son while there is hope, And do not set your heart on his destruction"* (Proverbs 19:18). In other words, if we as parents are afraid to discipline or correct our children, we are helping to destroy their lives, by encouraging their bad behavior. Likewise, how much more should our Heavenly Father chasten or correct us that He may turn us from the wrong path. Correction is so important—rather from God, parents or others—correction turns one from the road of destruction!

However, when we as God's children correct anyone, it should be with constructive or positive criticism. So, it is imperatives that we learn to speak words that produce a helpful healthy outcome in others, because that is what love does. Paul tells us in Ephesians 4:15 to *speak the truth in love* being careful not to damage or hurt the other person, that both, they and we may grow stronger and mature in Christ. Of course, some of us are more easily offended than others; because we may not be as mature as others, until we learn to love and rejoice even when we hear the truth about ourselves. Loving others and being truthful is not always easy, and can be painful and hard at times

Yes, people can hurt us and we can hurt people. In this life, we all make bad choices and we make mistakes, and sometimes we all just do stupid things, not because we don't love each other, but because we are flawed, imperfect human beings. Thank God, He loves us unconditionally, not for what we do, but because of who we are, we are His! And that is a wonderful thing to belong to the God of Grace, Love and Peace; with His willingness to forgive—giving us a second chance–again and again.

If you are not God's child yet—you need to open the door of your heart and invite Him in. He is near you right now, saying, *"Behold, I stand at the door and knock. If anyone hears My voice and opens the door, I will come in to him and dine with him, and he with Me" (Revelation 3:20)*. I guarantee you He will surely come in if you open the door of your heart and ask Him in. You don't have anything to lose, but you have everything to gain— your soul, forgiveness, heaven, peace, love, joy and His abiding presence! You may ask, 'how will I know or hear Him knock'? Well, one sure way to know—is when you have come to the end of yourself, and don't know what to do, or who to turn to. I would say, He is knocking!

Yes, love should not rejoice in iniquity, but rejoice in truth: and if truth set you free, what does a lie do—except hold you in bondage? And love certainly does not rejoice in bondage. Bondage causes one to feel weighted down and miserable. You may ask, what is bondage? Bondage is anything that keep, or hold you back from being free to rejoice in truth. It's a form of servitude or slavery to someone or something. It's the many situations, people and circumstances in our lives that we allow to oppress, depress, and suppress us. In short, bondage is wrong thinking, wrong believing, wrong feelings that keeps us held hostage, and interferes with our daily activities.

We can also have too much false information, or we just simply do not understand things as we should. Thus, causing our minds to be confused and our hearts to be heavy. Said another way, bondage is when we come under the control or influence of someone or something. That's why God wants us to know the truth so we can live our lives freely. So, take note of who are what you are listening to, and what you tell yourself? Do you tell yourself what God says about you? Do you tell yourself all the negative things the devil speaks about you? He likes to intimidate us by keeping our mind focused on negative situations. Remember the devil is the accuser and likes to keep us in bondage with all his lies. Whose report will you believe? God's, His Word, or the lies of the prince of this world (Ephesians 2:2)? Let's fortify ourselves with God's Word and tell Satan where he can go!

Thus, no worries, listen to what Jesus said He came to do––to set the captive free and to give us life more abundantly, He said, *"The thief does not come except to steal, and to kill, and to destroy. I have come that they may have life, and that they may have it more abundantly," (John 10:10).* Then He said in the book of Luke, *"The Spirit of the LORD is upon Me, Because He has anointed Me To preach the gospel to the poor; He has sent Me to* <u>*heal the brokenhearted, To proclaim liberty to the captives And recovery of sight to the blind, To set at liberty those who are oppressed;*</u> *To proclaim the acceptable year of the LORD." (Luke 4:18-19).*

So, Jesus has come to set the hostages, or the captives free; you and me; and the acceptable year of the Lord was a year of blessing, liberation, forgiveness, and a fresh start. In other words, a year to be set free and rejoice! So, lets rejoice in love and truth and open the door of our hearts wide for more of Jesus. He said, *"I am the door: by me if any man enters in, he shall be saved, and shall go in and out, and find pasture" (John10:9).* A pasture is like a Greengrass Meadowland, which is a good, restful and peaceful place to be. Amen!

Listen to the Lord's precious call. *"Come to Me, all you who labor and are heavy laden, and I will give you rest. Take My yoke upon you and learn from Me, for I am gentle and lowly in heart, and you will find rest for your souls. For My yoke is easy and My burden is light" (Matthew 11:28).* Coming to Jesus is the best and most important thing you can ever do for yourself and your family! Say this short simple prayer earnestly from your heart.

Lord, I accept Your invitation. I have sinned, forgive me, save me and make me your,' and show me what You want me to do, and I will serve You! Help me learn to love You and my fellow brothers and sisters. In Jesus name I pray this prayer–Amen!

Chapter 7

Love Bears All Things

...*"Bears all things, believes all things, hopes all things, endures all things" (I Co 13:7).*

There is a God. He is alive. *"For in Him we live and move and we survive and have our being" (Acts 17:28).* If I didn't know that God is, I would believe that He is; but I know that He is, because I am. He is the only One who can stand, bear, tolerate, stomach, suffer, stand, allow, accept, and endure all things. He put up with all our ugliness: jealousy disobedient, corruption, wickedness, destruction and perverse ways, selfishness, greed, immorality pridefulness, and all our other evil ways, and yet He still love us unconditionally. If that's not Love making the world go round–I don't know what is!

You see, *"For by Him all things were created that are in heaven and that are on earth, visible and invisible, whether thrones or dominions or principalities or powers. All things were created through Him and for Him. And He is before all things, and in Him all things consist" (Colossians 1:16-17).* All things mean you, me and everybody and everything else in the world. He created the world of spirits, the different orders of created intelligences, authorities, rules or the power that be. He created the whole universe of things, and upholds all things by the power of His Word. *"Who being the brightness of His glory and the express image of His person, and upholding all things by the word of His power, when He had by Himself purged our sins, sat down at the right hand of the Majesty on high" (Hebrews 1:3).* He is inevitably and undeniably God all by Himself—needing no other gods, and there is none like Him.

Listen to what God said, *"I am the LORD, and there is no other, there is no God beside me: I will gird you, though you have not known me" (Isaiah 45:5).* Then He said, *"Remember the former things of old: for I am God, and there is no other; I am God, and there is none like me" (Isaiah 46:9).* Love, God can undergo, suffer, endure or experience any and everything. Of Course, because He is God. But what about us as His children? Well, since God lives in us in the presence of the Holy Spirit—He empowers us with the ability, strength and courage to endure our difficult situations and tough circumstances when we rely on Him, and trust in Him.

He said He will never leave us nor forsake us; and He won't. God wants His children to love Him, believe Him, trust Him and know that He is our God. He wants us to be strong, unafraid and of good courage because we will have trouble as long as we live in this world. Listen to what He said to Joshua— these same words apply to us too. *"Have I not commanded you? Be strong and of good courage; do not be afraid, nor be dismayed, for the LORD your God is with you wherever you go." "Man that is born of a woman is of few days, and full of trouble" (Joshua 1:9, Job 14:1).* If God is with us where ever we go—He is with us whatever we go through—when we are fearful, heartbroken, sick, troubled, confused, depressed, worried, lonely, broken, disappointed, happy or sad—He is there.

However, we need to get to know Him so we will have no doubt that He is absolutely with us. God has already opened the door for us to approach Him when He sent Jesus to die for our sins. Jesus came and bridged the gap between God and man. Now, we can boldly approach His throne through prayer; and He will hear and answer us. He said, *"Call to Me, and I will answer you, and show you great and mighty things, which you do not know (Jeremiah 33:3).* Paul said, *"Let us therefore come boldly to the throne of grace, that we may obtain mercy and find grace to help in time of need" (Hebrews) 4:16.* Then Paul goes on to tell us to pray always, and to pray without ceasing (Eph 6:18, 1Th 5:17). So, you need to establish a personal relationship with God and get to know Him. He is right there inside you. Waiting for you to get to know Him. He is Real; rather you believe it or know it or not!

So, when trouble comes or things get too hard and it seems you can't make it, just call Him! He is a prayer away. He said, *"Then you will call upon Me and go and pray to Me, and I will listen to you" (Jeremiah 29:12)*. Yes, God listens to our prayers. He will bring you out of your distress and suffering, and give you strength, peace, and help you to walk upright with a feeling of love, joy and hope; and hope gives us the confidence for change.

Not only does God want us to endure tests, trials and tribulations, but He also wants us to hope all things and believe all things. Hope and believe the best in others, that all will turn out well, even when others have ceased to hope and believe. He wants us to be hopeful in all situations instead of despairing; believing instead of doubting. at least till the opposite appears, because that's what love does. When we have confidence in someone or something, we are not skeptical and suspicious, but trusting. The idea is to learn to look for the bright or positive side in every situation. Once the opposite view does appear, there is yet a loving appropriate way to approach the person or situation; especially if you are the one who was wronged.

Paul, the great apostle tells us exactly how to deal with such situations. He says, *"Repay no one evil for evil. Have regard for good things in the sight of all men. If it is possible, as much as depends on you, live peaceably with all men" (Romans 12:17-18)*.

"Now we exhort you, brethren, warn those who are unruly, comfort the fainthearted, uphold the weak, be patient with all. See that no one renders evil for evil to anyone, but always pursue what is good both for yourselves and for all" (1 Thessalonians 5:14-51).

In any event, our job as God children is to always exhibit love; and not hold grudges or try to get revenge on anyone: That's God's job. The Bible says, in proverbs *20:22, "Do not say, "I will recompense evil"; Wait for the LORD, and He will save you." "For we know Him who said, "Vengeance is Mine, I will repay," says the Lord. And again, "The LORD will judge His people"* (not us) *(Hebrews 10:30).* Our obedience to God begins with humility. We must believe that His way is better than our own. We may not always understand His ways of working, but by humbly trusting and obeying Him, we will receive His blessing.

God is always expressing His love to us through His grace and His mercy. He keeps giving us chance after chance; therefore, He wants us to show love to others by giving them chances, grace and mercy too. The Bible says, love covers all sins, and hatred stirs up strife, (Proverbs 10:12). So, we must practice choosing love over hate, and peace over strife, if we are to endure all things, hope all things, believe all things and bear all things; and love one another as He loves us all, for God is Love. *"God shows no partiality" (Acts 10:34),* and He has no respect of person.

I remember a time my family and I were sitting around the kitchen table having Bible Study; discussing 'people's attitudes.' God cut right in and I heard Him say, **"You accept people faults and all, or not at all."** I vividly realized how true that was. I saw clearly how God loves us with our imperfect selves; and how we can't accept a person's good without accepting the bad. Otherwise, we will have no one to love, or accept. *For all have sinned, and fall short of God's glory (Romans 3:23),* and we all are flawed, faulty and defective in one area or another.

It's the same when it comes to life situations; we can't accept good times without accepting bad times too. We must accept both sides of a situation. Just as we can't choose half of a person, as if to say I accept your good side, but I can't accept your bad side. No! We must choose to accept and love the whole person, the good, faults and all, or not at all, just like God said. However, we do not have to agree with their bad behavior or wrongdoing.

So, choosing to love, is choosing God, choosing God, is choosing Life! He wants us to choose life and live that we may be blessed, and be a blessing to our offspring and others. God desires the best for us and our families. What God told Joshua and the children of Israel yesteryear still applies to His children today. Listen to how strongly God feels about our love, obedience and worship to Him.

He said, *"See, I have set before you today life and good, death and evil, in that I command you today to love the LORD your God, to walk in His ways, and to keep His commandments, His statutes, and His judgments, that you may live and multiply; and the LORD your God will bless you in the land which you go to possess. But if your heart turns away so that you do not hear, and are drawn away, and worship other gods and serve them, I announce to you today that you shall surely perish; you shall not prolong your days in the land which you cross over the Jordan to go in and possess. I call heaven and earth as witnesses today against you, that I have set before you life and death, blessing and cursing; therefore choose life, that both you and your descendants may live; that you may love the LORD your God, that you may obey His voice, and that you may cling to Him, for He is your life and the length of your days;"* (Deuteronomy 30:15-20).

God lays it all out plainly in those verses making it clear on how we should live and act toward Him. Now that God has set both choices before us, and has told us to choose life so we could live; How will you choose? The Bible says, *"No one can serve two masters; for either he will hate the one and love the other, or else he will be loyal to the one and despise the other. You cannot serve God and mammon* (money*)." (Matthew 6:24).* So, let's choose God, love obedience and life that we ourselves, our families and others may live.

Did you know when God looks at you, He does not even waist His time looking at the color of your skin, but He takes great pleasure in looking at a pure heart? God does not even look to see if you are Jew or Gentile, rich or poor, black or white, educated or uneducated or male or female, but He does look to see if you are a person who loves and believe in Him, or, if you are a person who does not love and believe in Him; *for we are all one in Christ Jesus (Galatians 3; 28)*. There are No big I's and little you's; and no one better than another, for we are all His product. It looks like time is winding down from the way things looks in the world today; maybe you better make up your mind who you are going to serve; for times waits for no one.

Chapter 8

Every Thing Fails, but Love

..."*Love never fails. But whether there are prophecies, they will fail; whether there are tongues, they will cease; whether there is knowledge, it will vanish away*". *(I Co 13:8).*

God has given us all certain gifts and talents, enabling us to do somethings uniquely different from anyone else; and some of us are very gifted and extremely talented. Though we have faith to move mountains and able to retain and articulate great Knowledge and prophesy like Moses, and do miracles like Jesus; but all that greatness does not matter if we do not have love for God and our fellow brothers and sisters. Why? because all our greatness, our gifts, prophesying, knowledge or anything else we value will vanish away one day, everything as we know it will fail; it will cease to exist, stop functioning, it will be no more. But God's Word says love will never fail or cease to exist, because

Love is eternal, why? because God is LOVE, and God is eternal, from everlasting to everlasting, Love is unfailing and will continue throughout all eternity, for Love is of God.

Not only is Love of God, God is also Spirit and they that worship God *must worship Him in spirit and in truth. (John 4:24).* But before anyone can worship God, they must first believe that He is, and have faith and confidence that He truly exists. For His Word says, *"But without faith it is impossible to please Him: for he that cometh to God must believe that He is, and that He is a rewarder of them that diligently seek Him (Hebrews 11:6).*

So, God is Spirit as well as eternal. If God is Spirit, then so is our spirit eternal too. Therefore, when we die, we really don't die. Our spirit just separates from our physical bodies. In other words, our bodies go into the ground and our *spirit will return back to God Who gave it (Ecclesiastes 12:7).* Said this way, your spirit cannot die because it is eternal as God is eternal. May I strongly suggest that you take time out of your day and seek out your God and Creator while you still have time. Because one day you WILL die and leave your physical body behind: so please make sure you know where your spirit/soul will go. It can only go to one of two places—Heaven or Hell! No in between! (Matt 25:46).

Think about this. If God is in us, and we are in Him as Jesus made it very clear in the following scriptures when He was praying to God the Father—referring to His disciples, and us, He prayed, *"That they all may be one, as You, Father, are <u>in Me, and I in You</u>; that they also may <u>be one in Us</u>, that the world may believe that You sent Me. And the glory which You gave Me I have given them, that they may be <u>one just as We are one: I in them, and You in Me;</u> that they may be made perfect in one, and that the world may know that You have sent Me, and have loved them as You have loved Me"* (John 17:21-23). Amen! So, God's Spirit is in you rather you know it, understand it, or believe it or not. But more importantly—we belong to God; we are not our own. You might not know, understand or believe that either; but it's unquestionable and undeniably true.

Listen to His Word. *"Or do you not know that your body is the temple of the Holy Spirit who is in you, whom you have from God, and you are not your own"* (1 Corinthians 6:19). *"Do you not know that you are the temple of God and that the Spirit of God dwells in you? (1 Corinthians 3:16). "For you are the temple of the living God. As God has said: I will dwell in them And walk among them. I will be their God, And they shall be My people"* (11 Corinthians 6:16). You see, when God created us, He put His eternal Spirit inside us as the gift of life, creating us in His image. Then He gave us the choice to choose eternal life, and to love Him enough to live our life His way. He also gave us the choice to choose eternal death by rejecting Him by not living life His way.

You see, your soul cannot die, but it can suffer or endure eternal torment in hell forever; as it will experience eternal love in heaven forever, because your soul is the lifeforce, essence, or the core part of the human being that lives on eternally or forever. The soul is everlasting as God lives forever, from everlasting to everlasting. Not born, Never dying,' He is self-existing! Great God Almighty! YOU LIVE!

Just listen as you read the few scriptures below how Mighty, Awesome, Powerful, Real and Eternal our God really is. He is forever and ever and ever. He is endless! He is evermore: ceaselessly, forever, continually and unendingly from everlasting to everlasting. His love is worthy to behold, He is worthy to be praised and His power is worthy to be feared. Listen: hear the depth and power in the words of these verses. *"Blessed be the LORD God of Israel From everlasting to everlasting! And all the people said, "Amen!" and praised the LORD" (1 Chronicles 16:36). "Before the mountains were brought forth, Or ever You had formed the earth and the world, Even from everlasting to everlasting, You are God" (Psalms 90:2). "And many of those who sleep in the dust of the earth shall awake, Some to everlasting life, Some to shame and everlasting contempt" (Daniel 12:2). "And these will go away into everlasting punishment, but the righteous into eternal life" (Matthew 25:46). "But the mercy of the LORD is from everlasting to everlasting On those who fear Him, And His righteousness to children's children" (Psalms 103:17).*

God is a generational God and is always with His children. Just as He was with the prophets of old, His Son Jesus and many others in times past, so is He with us today. He changes not. He is the same yesterday, today and forever (Hebrews 3:8). As you continue reading–hear the depth of His power. Listen to this, *"Do not marvel at this; for the hour is coming in which all who are in the graves will hear His voice and come forth--those who have done good, to the resurrection of life, and those who have done evil, to the resurrection of condemnation" (John 5:28-29). "They will perish, but You remain; And they will all grow old like a garment; Like a cloak You will fold them up, And they will be changed. But You are the same, And Your years will not fail" (Hebrews 1:11-12).*

God's years will not fail, because He Is Love and Love will Never, Never Fail. Listen farther to how great He is: *"Lift up your eyes to the heavens, And look on the earth beneath. For the heavens will vanish away like smoke, The earth will grow old like a garment, And those who dwell in it will die in like manner; But My salvation will be forever, And My righteousness will not be abolished" (Isaiah 51:6),* Wow! Nothing can stop or eliminate God's justice from taking place, and nothing can eradicate or end God's rescue plan for His people!

God is Good all the time, and all the time God is good. He is Righteous, Fair and Just; nothing will stop Him from executing justice to those who reject Him. We will reap whatsoever we have sown! So, let us Love one another and do good deeds and sow good seeds. I, like my Father don't want to see anyone perish for rejecting Him, or for a lack of disobedience or un belief. God tells us through the Apostle Peter saying, *"The Lord is not slack concerning His promise, as some count slackness, but is longsuffering toward us, not willing that any should perish but that all should come to repentance" (2 Peter 3:9)*. Please, hear His Words and do not be too proud to humble yourself and repent! You won't regret it. You will only be glad you did!

Even in the New Testament Jesus Himself shows His obedience to His Father God and testifies to God's eternalness and everlastings existence, saying. *"And this is the will of Him who sent Me, that everyone who sees the Son and believes in Him may have everlasting life; and I will raise him up at the last day" (John 6:40)*. He said, *"Most assuredly, I say to you, he who believes in Me has everlasting life" (John 6:47)*. Jesus spoke what His Father spoke, saying, *"And I know that His command is everlasting life. Therefore, whatever I speak, just as the Father has told Me, so I speak" (John 12:50)*. If Jesus humbled Himself and showed His obedience to the Almighty God, shouldn't we also all the more?

Paul said this concerning God being everlasting, *"These shall be punished with everlasting destruction from the presence of the Lord and from the glory of His power," (II Thessalonians 1:9)*. In another place he says, *"For he who sows to his flesh will of the flesh reap corruption, but he who sows to the Spirit will of the Spirit reap everlasting life" (Galatians 6:8)*. So, here again we can see what happens when we sow or live according to our flesh; we also see what happens when we choose to sow or live our lives according to the Spirit of God. It seems those who obey not the gospel, there can be no end of their wickedness, and their destruction continues as they harden their hearts and are driven farther and farther away, or cut off from God's presence.

Paul says further that, *"The wicked man does deceptive work, But he who sows righteousness will have a sure reward. As righteousness leads to life, So he who pursues evil pursues it to his own death. Those who are of a perverse heart are an abomination to the LORD, But the blameless in their ways are His delight. Though they join forces, the wicked will not go unpunished; But the posterity of the righteous will be delivered"* *(Proverbs 11:1821)*. So, as we see, our life choices depend on our final destination; lets choose Jesus and the gospel. Please!

I tell you, if I didn't believe in God, I would surely believe in His powerfulness after reading these scriptures, since He is the only One Who has the power over my soul once it leaves my body. Listen to Jesus' warning, *"And do not fear those who kill the body but cannot kill the soul. But rather fear Him who is able to destroy both soul and body in hell"* *(Matthew 10:28)*. He says it a little differently in Luke, *"But I will show you whom you should fear: Fear Him who, after He has killed, has power to cast into hell; yes, I say to you, fear Him!"* *(Luke 12:5)*. The best thing we could ever do for ourselves is *humble ourselves under the mighty hand of God,* and repent of our sins, or wrongdoings (I Peter 5:6).

James says the same thing–giving us some hope; He said, *"Humble yourselves in the sight of the Lord, and he shall lift you up" (James 4:10)*. James is saying, if we submit to our God, He will raise us up. So, let's do our part. If we don't willingly submit to God, we may find ourselves in a situation where we have to unwillingly submit to Him. Listen to what God has said, *"I have sworn by Myself; The word has gone out of My mouth in righteousness, And shall not return, That to Me every knee shall bow, Every tongue shall take an oath" (Isaiah 45:23)*. Wow! Those words should make us a little fearful. But really the only thing we should fear anyway—is not having God in our lives!

Yes, God is the God of unconditional perfect love, but He warns us of that great and awful day of His wrath to come; (Zephaniah 1:14, Revelation 6:17, Jude 1:6, Revelation 16:14) giving us time to choose to repent of our sins and misdeeds, which is to turn from our evil, rebellious, wicked and malicious ways. He is also giving us time to learn how to love others, and forgive them, *for we all have sinned and fall short of the glory of God (Romans 3:23)*.

The Bible says if we have love we are born of God, and God is in us. The book of John states, *"Beloved, let us love one another, for love is of God; and everyone who loves is born of God and knows God" (1 John 4:7)*. Paul said, *"But if anyone loves God, he is known by God" (1 Corinthians 8:3)*. Does God know you by the love you show toward others? What have you done to genuinely help someone else lately? Peter lets us know

82

how very importance love is by saying, *"Above all, keep loving one another earnestly, since love covers a multitude of sin, Be hospitable to one another without grumbling,"* (1 Peter 4:8-9). And Paul says, *"Let brotherly love continue,"* (Hebrews 13:1). We should all work toward being of one mind and heart: Feel for one another, comfort one another, support one another; and remember that he who professes to love God should love his brother also. Stated another way, when we truly love someone, we desire the best for them. We don't hold their sins, faults, mistakes, shortcoming or failures against them, but we are soon to forgive, for we too are also guilty of something.

You may ask, how do I show more love to other? Glad you asked. By doing good deeds to help up-lift their spirit in some way. Any good thing you do for others is helping to build up the Kingdom of God:

- Try smiling at, or speaking more to others.
- Pray for someone you know who is in trouble
- Visit someone you know that doesn't feel well.
- Give monthly to a charity that needs support.
- Buy food for someone in need of it.
- Keep someone's children for a day.
- Bake cookies or cook a meal for someone.
- Take a needy person shopping.
- Give a word of encouragement.
- Give financial support, not to get it back.

- Provide shelter for one who need it.
- Provide transportation for someone.
- Or do whatever you are able to do that you want to do. Just get in the habit of showing a little more love to others.

Paul said, *"And now abide faith, hope, love, these three; but the greatest of these is love" (1 Corinthians 13:13)*. Love is the greatest, for love is the sum of perfection on earth; love alone is the sum of perfection in heaven. Our faith strengthens our walk with God. Our hope gives us confidence in God and help us believe in him and expect His blessing. So having faith, hope and love is the sure way to live fruitfully and successfully. The Spirit of God does indeed abide in God's children. Even Jesus tells us to abide in Him as He abide in us. Abide means to live in, or live with, or stay with, or to dwell within.

Listen to what Jesus says to us concerning abiding in Him, He said, *"Abide in Me, and I in you. As the branch cannot bear fruit of itself, unless it abides in the vine, neither can you, unless you abide in Me" (John 15:4)*. And again, He said, *"At that day you will know that I am in My Father, and you in Me, and I in you" (John 14:20)*. God the father Himself said, *"....I will dwell in them And walk among them. I will be their God, And they shall be My people" (2 Corinthians 6:16)*. In this following verse Jesus was praying to His Father about us. He prayed, *"That they all may be one, as You, Father, are in Me, and I in You; that they also may be one in Us, that the world may believe that You sent Me"*

(John 17:21). It can't get any clearer than that; our God lives in us and we live in Him! But best of all, He love us unconditionally and He is just a prayer away. You can call on Him anytime, day or night, He'll be there!

Sense God is Love, and God is in us, then we have love too, we just have to make more room in our hearts for Him. Therefore, we really need to understand that without God, we are nothing. Living according to the morals and values of this world can easily cause us to become puffed up and prideful, thinking that we don't need God, causing us to feel as if we are in charge and have accomplished all that we have on our own; when in reality, it is God Who has accomplished it through us. It is He Who has given us the power to get wealth, for by His Spirit, *we live and move and have our being in Him (De 8:18, Ac 17:28)*.

So beware, following the standards of this present world will take you farther than you want to go and keep you longer than you want to stay—making your life miserable. Know that God can withdraw His Spirit or breath from our bodies whenever He gets ready and there is nothing, we can do about it; except be ready when He does.

So, love never fail, because God never fails, and both God and Love are unfailing. Said another way, God can do anything, but FAIL! So, let's all just make up our minds to let God be Himself through us. Lets' make up our minds to love God more, so we can become lovers of others more. Love comes from God;

He gave us Jesus; He is the Founder and giver of love. *"For God so loved the world that He sent His only begotten Son, that whosoever believe in Him should not perish but have ever lasting life" (John 3:16).* Do you believe?

God sent His Son because He loved us so much. He wanted to deliver us and save us from a life of bondage of sin and evil works of the flesh; such as wickedness, corruption, darkness, immorality, hatred, jealousy, strife, bitterness, depression, dishonesty, envy, hostility, malice, fear, confusion, anger, adultery, fornication, resentment, distresses, worry, wrath, drunkenness, crime, and even from ourselves, from going crazy, and all other evils and negativity Satan loves to burden us with. Nevertheless, God want His children to live burden free according to the fruit of the Spirit; which are love, joy, peace, forgiveness, gentleness, kindness, goodness, faithfulness, meekness, compassion, mercy, grace, temperance, longsuffering and self-control (Galatians 5:22-23). You see, the fruit of the Spirit are the attributes or characteristics of our God.

Jesus's life on earth demonstrated to us how we are to live out those characteristics. Being a Learner and Follower of Jesus makes living life so much easier. He has invited all saying, *"Come to Me, all you who labor and are heavy laden, and I will give you rest. Take My yoke upon you and learn from Me, for I am gentle and lowly in heart, and you will find rest for your souls. For My yoke is easy and My burden is light" (Matt 11:28).* Don't you want rest for your weary soul? His burdens are truly lighter than the weight the world tries to put on our shoulders. Jesus' yoke/burden is freedom from the weight and bondage of this world. All you have to do is accept Him and believe what He has done for you.

Listen to these verses. *"For God did not send His Son into the world to condemn the world, but that the world through Him might be saved. He who believes in Him is not condemned; but he who does not believe is condemned already, because he has not believed in the name of the only begotten Son of God. And this is the condemnation, that the light has come into the world, and men loved darkness rather than light, because their deeds were evil. For everyone practicing evil hates the light and does not come to the light, lest his deeds should be exposed. But he who does the truth comes to the light, that his deeds may be clearly seen, that they have been done in God"* *(John 3:17-20).* Amen! We should be grateful and thankful to God every day, because He loved us enough to send Jesus to show us the way back to Him.

When someone does not want to hear anything about what we have to say about God or Jesus, could it be that they have evil thoughts in their hearts/minds; could it be that they have evil works in their life and are afraid they may be exposed? Could it be because those who love truth come to the light, and have a life that was changed and others don't like it? Or, could it be because many have been cleverly deceived by the prince of the power of the air, walking according to this world in sin and iniquity; or walking according to the works of the flesh?

You see, we who are saved now were once dead in trespasses living in disobedience to God's standard; living according to the ways of this world too, but Jesus has quickened our spirits together with Him, now we are learners and followers of Christ. Listen, *"Wherein in time past ye walked according to the course of this world, according to the prince of the power of the air, the spirit that now worketh in the children of disobedience" (Ephesians 2:1-2).* We were there too once. But Jesus has changed our lives. Now our assignment from God is to Help you come to Jesus—coming to truth, light and life *more abundantly* (John 10:10).

No matter the reason others may not want to hear anything about God or Jesus—we must remember to do as the Apostle Paul directed young Timothy to do, because we shouldn't argue or try forcing truth on anyone. He said, *"But avoid foolish and ignorant disputes, knowing that they generate strife. And a servant of the Lord must not quarrel but be gentle to all, able to teach, patient, in humility correcting those who are in opposition, if God perhaps will grant them repentance, so that they may know the truth, and that they may come to their senses and escape the snare of the devil, having been taken captive by him to do his will" (2 Timothy 2:23-26).*

God has sent Jesus, saying, *"I am the way, the truth, and the life. No one comes to the Father except through Me" (John 14:6).* He came to save us, comfort, guide, teach and lead us from this dark, fallen, confused, depraved, perverse, corrupt and crooked world's perspective—into God's marvelous light. *In Him was life, and the life was the light of men,* that we may learn how to live and walk in the ways of our Lord and God, (John 1:4).

Before Jesus went back home to heaven to be with His Father, He told us saying, *"Yor are the salt of the earth; ...You are the light of the world. A city that is set on a hill cannot be hidden". (Matthew 5:13-14).* Since our life, light and love cannot be hidden from this dark world, let's let it shine as bright as we can through acts of love through good deeds, mercy, forgiveness and compassion.

Peter said, *"But you are a chosen generation, a royal priesthood, a holy nation, His own special people, that you may proclaim the praises of Him who called you out of darkness into His marvelous light" (1 Peter 2:9).* Paul said, *"...God chose us in Him before the foundation of the world, that we should be holy and without blame before Him in love" (Ephesians 1:4).* John said, *"But whoever keeps His word, truly the love of God is perfected in him. By this we know that we are in Him" (John 2:5).* When we love our brothers and sisters, we know that, not only does God love us, but God is in us and we are in God!

The reason why Paul has emphasized the importance of 'Love' is because 'Love' is of God and it never fail. However, he says what will fail. *"But whether there are prophecies, they will fail; whether there are tongues, they will cease; whether there is knowledge, it will vanish away" (1 Corinthians 13:8).* But not "LOVE." He says further–putting more emphases on 'Love,' saying, *"And now abide faith, hope, Love, these three; but the greatest of these is 'Love" (1Co 13:13).* Love is the greatest of all human qualities and is a major attribute of God Himself. Love involves unselfish service to others. Jesus said the greatest among us are those of us who serve, and serve with love. *"But he who is greatest among you shall be your servant"* (Matthew 23:11). Besides yourself, who do you serve, help, aid, support, assist or provide relief for?

So, again, Love never, never fails, because love is unfailing; and as long as we as God's children continue to love as He commanded us to, the world will continue to go round. Because Love was here before the world. Love always was in the world, Love always is in the world, and Love always will be in the world, for LOVE created the world, *"for God so loved the world that He gave His only begotten Son, that whoever believes in Him should not perish but have everlasting life (John 3:16).*

The surest way to experience God's great Unconditional Love is to truly get to know your Creator and God by making Him your focal point as you move through your daily life; for the only way any of us can keep our balance is to keep our eyes on God, the One Who never changes. Because if we don't keep our eyes on Him our circumstances and situations will seem to be spinning around us nonstop, and we will surely slip away. However, we will stay settle, steady, solid, stable secure, and safe when we keep our focus on our loving God above, yet, Who is also residing within His children here below in the presence of the Holy Spirit.

In the meanwhile, do not be too alarm by all the terrible things that are going on in the world right now; just make God your Creator your major focus, and get to know Him because you need Him–rather you know it or not. For it appears the last days are definitely here. know that the Bible is being fulfilled every day right before our eyes. The prophets of old, Jesus and the apostles have already prophesied or predicted that these dangerous and unsafe times would come in the last days. So, take heed to the warning signs and seek God for peace and comfort. Because things are not going to get better, but rest assured, God has it all in complete control.

In conclusion, I quote the Apostle Paul in the words he told young Timothy, saying, *"But know this, that in the last days perilous times will come: For men will be lovers of themselves, lovers of money, boasters, proud, blasphemers, disobedient to parents, unthankful, unholy, unloving, unforgiving, slanderers, without self-control, brutal, despisers of good, traitors, headstrong, haughty, lovers of pleasure rather than lovers of God." "For the time will come when they will not endure sound doctrine; but after their own lusts shall they heap to themselves teachers, having itching ears; And they shall turn away their ears from the truth, and shall be turned unto fables," (2 Timothy 3:1-4, 2 Timothy 4:3-4).* These scriptures certainly describe the mindset and conditions that are presently in the world today. Do you think it's time to make your choice?

Father, I pray we all become seekers and lovers of You more, rather than seekers and lovers of our own things. *"For all seek their own, not the things which are of Christ Jesus" (Philippians 2:21).* Let us seek to lift up love, and love will continue to lift us up; for love helps when nothing else can, because God is Love.

Love makes The World Go Round

LOVE LIFTED ME

"I was sinking deep in sin, far from the peaceful shore,
Very deeply stained within, sinking to rise no more;
But the Master of the sea heard my despairing cry,
From the waters lifted me, now safe am I.

Love lifted me! Love lifted me!
When nothing else could help,
Love lifted me.
Love lifted me! Love lifted me!
When nothing else could help,
Love lifted me.

All my heart to Him I give, ever to Him I'll cling,
In his blessed presence live, ever his praises sing.
Love so mighty and so true merits my soul's best songs;
Faithful loving service, too, to Him belongs. [Refrain]

Souls in danger, look above, Jesus completely saves;
He will lift you by His love out of the angry waves;
He's the master of the sea, billows His will obey;
He your Savior wants to be, be saved today.

Love lifted me! Love lifted me! When nothing else could help,
Love lifted me. Love lifted me. When nothing else could help,"

Song written by, James Rowe

94

For Others Books

by Taliba Lockhart

contact information:
https://faithbuildingbooks.com
www.amazon.com/author/talibalockhart

Please feel free to comment, ask questions, or if you have concerns: email tallock48@gmail.com

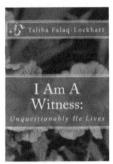

$12.00

$14.00

$14.00

$14.00

$$14.00

$9.00

$9.00

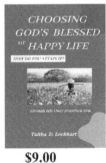

$9.00

$14.00

GOD IS LOVE

What the world needs now is Love sweet Love,
God is the only One people just doesn't get enough of.
What the world needs now is Love, sweet Love.
No, He is not just for some, but God is for everyone!

I am just a pointer, pointing to the POINTER

And I pray God strengthen and help us all *be not conformed to this world, but* continue to *be transformed by the renewing of our minds, that we may prove what is that good and acceptable and perfect will of God (Romans 12:2).*

The Purpose For this Book

My only intent for writing this book is to help others come to know the Awesome Depth and Power of our Almighty Living God, and His Unconditional Perfect Love for His children, and how much He wants us to learn how to love one another.

$14.00

Made in the USA
Columbia, SC
12 November 2022

71057126R00075